THE POET'S KIT

How to work

with the

elements of poetry

KATHERINE KNIGHT

Drawings by Jane Kingshill

PRAXIS BOOKS

Praxis Books
"Sheridan", Broomers Hill Lane, Pulborough,
West Sussex. RH20 2DU

Illustrations by Jane Kingshill

ISBN 0-9518729-5-8

British Library Cataloguing-in-Publication Data.
A catalogue record for this book is available from the British Library

Printed by Biddles Ltd. Guildford and King's Lynn.

For all my friends, past and present,
at the City Lit

ACKNOWLEDGEMENTS

For permission to reprint extracts, whole poems and other copyright material, grateful acknowledgement is made to the following publishers and other copyright holders:

Faber & Faber Ltd for 'Edward Lear', 'Night Mail', 'Anthem for St Cecilia's Day', 'Letter to Lord Byron' and 'The Sheild of Achilles' from *Collected Poems* by W.H.Auden edited by Edward Mendelson and 'Chorus' from *The Dog Beneath the Skin* by W.H.Auden and Christopher Isherwood. Also Faber & Faber Ltd for 'To My Mother' and 'The True Confession of George Barker', Book One (1950) from *Collected Poems* by George Barker. Also for 'Follower' from *Death of a Naturalist* by Seamus Heaney and for 'Full Moon and Little Frieda' from *Wodwo* by Ted Hughes and for 'The North Ship' from *The North Ship* by Philip Larkin; for extracts from 'Murder in the Cathedral' and 'The Waste Land' from *The Complete Poems and Plays of T.S.Eliot* and from 'Hamlet' in *Selected Essays* by T.S.Eliot. For 'Dublin' from *The Collected Poems* of Louis MacNiece edited by E.R. Dodds, 'Insomniac', 'Cut' and 'Mirror' from *Collected Poems* by Sylvia Plath edited by Ted Hughes; 'Alba' from *Collected Shorter Poems* by Ezra Pound; 'Memento' from *The Terrible Rain* by Steven Spender.

John Murray (Publishers) Ltd for 'Harvest Hymn' from *Collected Poems* by John Betjeman 1988 and 'Beachcomber' from *Selected Poems* by George Mackay Brown.

David Higham Associates for 'Ballad of the Bread Man' from *Collected Poems* of Charles Causley, Macmillan and for 'A Charm against the Toothache' from *A Charm against the Toothache* by John Heath-Stubbs, Methuen. Also for 'The Force that Through the Green Fuse drives the Flower', 'Fern Hill' and 'Once Below a Time' from *The Poems of Dylan Thomas*, Dent.

A.P.Watt Ltd on behalf of The Trustees of the Robert Graves Copyright Trust for 'Love without Hope' and 'Sick Love' from *Collected Poems 1975* by Robert Graves, Cassell.

Oxford University Press: 'The Lesson' by Edward Lucie-Smith from *A Tropical Childhood and Other Poems* (1961) by permission of Oxford University Press; 'Cathedral Builders' from *Definition of a Waterfall* by John Ormond (c) OUP 1973 by permission of Oxford University Press; 'A Martian Sends a Postcard Home', 'Shallots', 'The Trout Farm' and 'Memories of the Linen Room' from *A Martian Sends a Postcard Home* (1979) by Craig Raine by permission of Oxford University Press.

Random House UK Ltd and the Estate of Robert Frost for 'After Apple Picking' from *The Poetry of Robert Frost* edited by Edward Connery Lathem, Jonathan Cape. Also for 'Aunt Julia' and 'Movements' from *Collected Poems* by Norman MacCaig, Chatto & Windus 1990.

Carcanet Press Ltd for 'The Legacy' from *The Pleasure Steamers* by Andrew Motion 1978 and for 'Rain' by William Carlos Williams, from

Collected Poems of William Carlos Williams Vol I 1909–1939, Vol 2 1939–1962, New Directions, 1986, Carcanet 1988. Also for 'Thomas Müntzer III' from *Heart's Desire* by Jeffrey Wainwright 1978.
For a haiku by **Brian Cater** the author: from *The Haiku Hundred* Iron Press, 1992. **Peters Frazer & Dunlop Group Ltd** for 'Responsibilities' from *Poems* by Anthony Cronin, The Cresset Press 1957. 'my father moved through dooms of love' from *Complete Poems 1904–1962* by e.e.cummings, Copyright (c) 1968 Marion Morehouse Cummings. Reproduced with the permission of **W.W. Norton & Company.** For 'Instead of a Carol' by **Tom Earley** the author: from *Rebel's Progress*, Gomer Press 1979. **J.M. Dent & Sons** for 'Orpheus in the Underworld' from *Hölderlin's Madness* by David Gascoyne. ***New Statesman & Society*** for 'Cancer's a Funny Thing' by J.B.S. Haldane and 'Limeraiku' by Ted Pauker. For 'A Valentine for Ophelia' by **Jane Kingshill** the author. **Laurence Pollinger Ltd** and **Phyllis McGinley** for 'Reflections at Dawn' from *The Love Letters of Phyllis McGinley* Viking Penguin Inc. reprinted by permission of **Curtis Brown Ltd NY** 'The Cow' from *Free Wheeling* by Ogden Nash, Simon & Schuster, Little Brown and Co and 'Spring Song' from *I'm a Stranger Here Myself* by Ogden Nash, Simon & Schuster, Little Brown and Co. (c) 1931 and 1935. For 'My Northern-Sister' by **Grace Nichols** the author: from *The New Poetry* Bloodaxe Books 1993. **Reed Book Services Ltd** for 'The Return' from *Psyche and the Hurricane* by Michèle Roberts, Methuen (c) 1991 Michèle Roberts. For 'Jailbird' by **Vernon Scannell** the author: from *Mastering the Craft* Pergamon Press 1970. For 'Slow-Burning Autumn' by **John Smith** the author: from *Excursus in Autumn*, Hutchinson 1958. **James MacGibbon** for 'The Galloping Cat' from *The Collected Poems of Stevie Smith* (Penguin 20th Century Classics). **Macmillan London Ltd** for 'Poetry for Supper' from *Poetry for Supper* by R.S. Thomas. For 'Worm Within' by **Anthony Thwaite** the author: from *Poems 1953–1988*, Hutchinson 1989. The **Andrew Young Estate** for 'Autumn Mist', 'Last Snow' and 'A Dead Mole' from *The Poetical Works of Andrew Young* 1985, Secker & Warburg.

Praxis Books apologises for any errors or omissions in the above list and would be glad to hear of any corrections that should be included in further editions of this work. While every effort has been made to trace copyright holders, in one or two cases this has proved impossible.

CONTENTS

FOREWORD

For the past twelve years I have run an informal poetry writing club at the `City Lit' in Holborn, London. The City Literary Institute is a College of Adult Education, independent since 1990. It is open day and evening, six days a week, with a life-enhancing purpose. Here people pursue literature, foreign languages, music, drama, painting and other subjects conducive to pure happiness.

For a couple of hours a week, a dozen of us meet to listen to poems being read aloud (twice), then give helpful criticism and general feedback to each other.

Rules for writing are flexible, because live poetry outgrows constraints. We ask only *Does it come off? And if not, why not?* Nevertheless some people prefer to work with time-honoured versification, and any poet can do with a few hints from the best poems of the past. Others are concerned with breaking out of old cages, and share their exhilaration with the rest.

This book has grown out of these poems and discussions. It is meant for anyone who has started to write, or who would like to. There are no age limits because experience and exuberance go together in creating verse. I hope it will be as helpful to older people turning to poetry to express what they have learnt of life as to younger ones in their first enthusiasm.

The progressive exercises at the end of each chapter are adaptable and, I hope, fun to try. There is enough theory to explain how poetry works, and to enhance enjoyment of what you read, but the book is largely concerned with practice - the care, choice and sharpening of tools in the poet's kit.

CHAPTER 1

BRAINWAVES

Poetry is important.

To be human is to need art. Wherever there is a moment to spare from childcare or harvest, people turn to storytelling, dancing, music or picture-making. Even Western civilisation, criticised for being too materialistic, uses its technology to serve the same cause. Paperback fiction, pop, rock, Beethoven, the images of advertising, film and television satisfy this hunger whenever people take five minutes off work.

But poetry is special in that it contains elements of several arts. A poem often tells a story and always depends on some word-music and imagery for its effect. It is concentrated and needs full attention if it is to be appreciated intellectually, but often its truth is felt with a shiver of recognition - experienced, not analysed.

It may be that poetry gives pleasure in the same way as dancing or the perception of colour does. It has a physical, sensual aspect as well as intellectual meaning, appealing to the whole personality of the reader because it speaks to the two halves of the brain, which are believed to have different functions.

Generally speaking, the left cerebral hemisphere is specialised for language, logic and mathematics, as well as many other things. The right hemisphere seems to be largely non-verbal, but is the source of emotion, and the seat of artistic and musical talents. There is a complex system of exchange between the two halves, so that a person can (usually) function as a whole. Research on creativity, even scientific creativity, suggests that the right side contributes sudden insight, for which the methodical left has laid the foundations by research and questioning. After the 'flash of intuition' logic has to prepare a feasibility study. The whole brain is required to invent something valuable.

The same process must be true of writing - and reading - poetry. Language is obviously essential. The poet's left hemisphere must be crackling with electricity. But the rhythm and word-sounds of poetry are akin to music, which is a right brain function, as is the picture-making faculty of imagination. It is agreed that Western technology is a triumph of the scientific method, of logic and mathematics - largely left-brain work. But balance is essential. The right-brain is as necessary to being human as the left. The splitting Western head needs to be made whole. Poetry is important.

INSPIRATION

The poet's eye, in a fine frenzy rolling,
Doth glance from heaven to earth, from earth to heaven;
And, as imagination bodies forth
The forms of things unknown, the poet's pen
Turns them to shapes, and gives to airy nothing
A local habitation and a name.
(A Midsummer Night's Dream. V.i.)

Shakespeare, who knew so much, seems to confirm the process I have described. First imagination, then the pen. But a lot of hushed talk about 'genius', common in the past, discourages writers who want practical tips for improvement.

This was the story put about:-

The Poet, with capital P, long hair and quill pen, sits at a desk, frequently with bottle of Scotch, or equivalent, to hand. Behind him, half in shadow, a winged figure labelled 'Muse' is dictating the Immortal Work. The Poet is no more than a clerk, but that doesn't prevent his banking a cheque for royalties later. Those of you who cannot produce a perfect poem, first time, obviously have no inspirational Muse and would be better employed putting the pips in raspberry jam.

If anything like this ever occurs, the poet's right-brain has been busily thinking, though 'subconsciously' – without words.

When conditions are favourable, the poem's imagery and music harness the left-brain, where they are embodied in language. The poem almost writes itself. It seems miraculous. It probably happens most often to those who have already practised a great deal.

A modern idea, equally unhelpful, is that if a poem takes over and writes itself, it is sacrilege to alter a word of it.

Here are some practical ways of finding the poems inside you.

Donnée

Literally a 'gift'.

A common way to start. You may be doing something entirely different (bossy left-brain distracted, so the right can make a bid for attention). Suddenly an image, idea or a complete line comes 'into your head'. It may even come to you in a dream. This is the germ of the poem, sometimes the important first or last line.

When you come to explore this (and it is a mini-inspiration, to be treated respectfully), it is far better to try to make internal conditions good for the right-brain, not the left. You already have a signal that there is a poem waiting to be born. Follow the *General Rules* given below.

It is important to encourage yourself to respond to this kind of creativity. The spark may grow into a sparkler. Buy a small notebook, keep it with you wherever you are, and write down these thoughts immediately. If you don't, they get forgotten, like dreams. Preserve them, and you can follow them through at leisure. Also the act of recording will train you to recognise the feeling when there is a poem in the air.

Personal Experience

In one sense, all your poetry must come out of your own experience - where else could it come from? But in a particular instance, something very important may happen to you, such as falling in love or the death of a friend. You may witness or be involved in an accident, the birth of a child, a great success or a separation. Any strong emotion can impel you to write about its cause, circumstances and effects. So can more ordinary happenings. High drama may be quite unnecessary. For instance, a quiet evening stroll may be all you need, as here:-

AUTUMN

A touch of cold in the autumn night -
I walked abroad,
And saw the ruddy moon lean over a hedge,
Like a red-faced farmer.
I did not stop to speak, but nodded,
And round about were the wistful stars
With white faces like town children.

(T.E.Hulme)

Earnest, earthless, equal, attuneable, vaulty, voluminous,... stupendous
Evening strains to be time's vast, womb-of-all, home-of-all, hearse-of-all night.
Her fond yellow hornlight wound to the west, her wild hollow hoarlight hung to the height...

(G.M. Hopkins. from 'Spelt from Sibyl's Leaves')

If you have an eye for detail, and interest in the way things happen, you are already half-way to being a poet. Cultivate the eye and the interest. Paradoxically you need to know the particular individuality of things, and to speak honestly in your own voice and time in order to make a universal appeal.

Specific details make your poetry far more convincing than vague generalisations do, helping to persuade readers that they are sharing the experience or emotion you describe. With luck they will be reminded of broadly similar events or feelings, and so conclude that what you are saying is authentic and of personal relevance to them. If your mode of expression seems archaic, second-hand or difficult to enter into, the delicate illusion will vanish. There is more about this in Chapters Five and Seven.

Books, Magazines, Paintings, TV, Radio etc.

Experience can include your reading or TV viewing, and responding with a poem is just as appropriate as a response to an event happening directly to you.

There are several ways of treating other people's art. You can describe your own emotions - Keats's 'On First Looking Into Chapman's Homer' for instance. You can speak to the writer or painter, or describe the total effect of his work, as Auden does in 'Edward Lear':-

And children swarmed to him like settlers. He became a land.

Another way is to take the text or picture as the substance of your poem, picking out the important details, and converting them to images. One of the members of the Poetry Club I organise finds a new poem almost every day in the colour-supplements, TV documentaries or visits to art galleries. It is as if he steps inside the picture.

Radio items can be equally stimulating, as your imagination is already engaged in producing 'pictures' for the words you hear.

It is difficult to write this kind of poem with as much spontaneity as when responding to first-hand events. It tends to be more intellectual, less emotional, but you can compensate by taking extra care over originality of images and language.

Being Someone Else

There is no need whatever to confine yourself to your `real' personality when you write. To take on another character - a *persona* as it is called - gives you the freedom to explore in imagination whatever you wish. (Indeed, the power of poetry to heal and console may be partly due to this liberation.)

The female can speak with a male voice, or vice versa. You can be a saint or criminal, coward or heroine. You can visit other times, other cultures, other worlds if you want to. You can take an episode from your own life yet preserve your privacy by transferring it to some other person. Even if you write in the first person, the 'I' can wear a mask of any kind. You can even imagine yourself as an animal, or become stone, metal, water or sky.

Starting from Cold

There may be times when you want to write *something* but find yourself at the opposite pole to the inspired Poet, your mind as blank as the paper. In this predicament one of these approaches may help:

Words of Power Single words that have strong symbolic or emotional associations will sometimes act as keys to imagination. Sometimes they can be the title of the finished poem too. Such a list might include - *Sun, Bread, Stone, Blood, Water, Secrets, Earth...* A dictionary of symbols will give hundreds more. Having chosen one, either go on to the next procedure, or the *General Rules* below, which are to be followed no matter how the idea for a poem is found.

Free Association This is a polite way of requesting the subconscious to co-operate. Write down any word or phrase at all - chosen at random from a cornflakes-packet will do. As quickly as possible write down whatever comes next into your mind, and continue with the next, and so on. Spend five minutes on this, then look at the list to see if there is any pattern there. Commonly, some of the words will be rhymes, some synonyms, some obvious associations such as boot/shoe/sock. But an original theme may be found there too, shining in the middle of the garbage. Once more, follow the *General Rules.*

A variation is to put a word that carries emotion for you in the middle of a blank page, and write the associations round it, going back to the first word each time. Then add new associations to the first ones you thought of. Perhaps several of the thoughts belong together? If so, join them with arrows. Continue with promising phrases, new images and so on ... The finished page will look as if someone upset the dictionary all over the floor, but you may see the makings of a strongly individual poem.

Stream of Consciousness Similar to the above, but instead of a list you simply write, without stopping, for ten or fifteen minutes, whatever comes into your head. It's important to accept the thoughts as they come. True, they may turn out to be from your shadow side, unpleasant in some way, but such things have a lot of energy. Releasing them harmlessly onto paper can be therapeutic as well as interestingly self-revealing. You don't have to use this knowledge raw if you don't want to.

Equally well, this kind of writing can remind you of particular joys, dreams or hopes, hidden wisdom and odd facts. Equally well, too, it may be pretty trivial. 'I don't know what to say next. There's a fly on the window. I wish it was teatime. I wish I wasn't so fat ...' (Even so, this might give you the idea for a poem about a fat fly.)

Other People's Poems If you write poetry, you probably like reading it too. What you have read in the past will influence what you write now, though everyone develops an individual voice with practice. But you can use other people's poems deliberately, and legitimately, to give yourself ideas.

One way is to read a poem as if you were listening to a friend speaking. At some point you may want to argue, or at least to put another view. Perhaps the story reminds you of something that happened to you, or that you can imagine happening...Another way is to summarise it in the most general terms, then let this idea re-form using your own images. For instance, Edward Thomas's 'Adelstrop' is about an unscheduled stop in the countryside during a journey. Play with the 'unscheduled stop' idea. Car breakdown? Forced landing? Hijack of plane or ship? Where? Lonely road, night, desert; middle of town? Exotic land? Foreign harbour? Who else involved? No-one (like 'Adelstrop'), or someone helpful? Sinister? Terrorists? Pirates? Happy experience (like 'Adelstrop'), or sad, terrifying, comic or spooky? Already you may have ideas for a dozen poems.

The contents and index pages of an anthology will give you numerous titles and lines. Pick one – preferably belonging to a poem you haven't read yet. What poem of yours would have that title, or that first line? When you have written it, you can change the title, alter the line, and the poem becomes completely your own.

More obviously derivative, but still honest, is to write in the style of another poet, exaggerating mannerisms, or quoting enough of the original to make it recognisable. If you are witty enough, this will be a perfectly good parody. From your point of view it is best to choose a well-known poet and a good poem, but remember that parody can be destructive. Be prepared, one day, for someone to do the same to you!

If you know another language, translating a poem is another perfectly honourable way of using your own talent. It can also teach you a great deal because a translation ideally follows the original in poetic technique as well as meaning. (You must of course get permission before publishing a translation of work covered by copyright in another country.)

GENERAL RULES

Sit somewhere warm and comfortable, with silence or music as you prefer. (Though some people write very well on trains, perhaps because of the rhythmical rocking.)

If you meditate, this may be a way of calming down an over-enthusiastic left-brain for a little while before you begin.

For a preliminary draft, you may prefer to record on a cassette tape rather than writing.

Having got your general idea in mind, don't criticise or censor yourself, don't worry about the final form your poem will take, don't attempt to produce regular rhymes, rhythm or even bother about grammar or spelling.

Sit quietly and let images suggest themselves, Don't strive for originality. Just put words around the ideas. List single words or quick phrases if you experience a flood of imagery.

If you get stuck, return to your original idea and see if different associations will come. When you are tired, put the work away for a while. You may get more ideas as you do other things, letting the subconscious mind, or right-brain, continue to work on the poem in its own way. (It doesn't matter what you call it, as long as you trust it.)

NEVER talk about a poem, not even to your lover or your best friend, until you have written several drafts and need a second opinion. Expressing the emotion is conversation may discharge it prematurely, with no energy left for the poem.

Once you have the raw first draft, your poem will almost certainly need cooking, probably several times over. Read your poems aloud, or tape and listen to them, as part of the editing process. You can often hear where improvement is needed though you can't see it.

POEMS TO BEGIN

Please have a go at this practical work before reading the next chapter. This applies all through the book. The practice is cumulative, designed to enable you to build your skill with one tool at a time. Follow the 'General Rules' above as you do them.

1. Think back over the past six months of your life. What was the most important thing that happened to you, good or bad? Write the first draft of a poem about it, saying what happened and how you felt at the time.

2. Write another, describing how you feel now.

3. Using the same experience, write another, but this time speaking as if you were a witness not personally involved.

4. Find an attractive picture of a group of people, in an art gallery, magazine, book etc. Write a rough draft of a poem to explain why it appeals to you. Include enough description

to give an idea of the picture to someone who hasn't seen it.

5. Using the same picture, imagine you are one of the people shown. Produce another draft explaining the situation in which you find yourself. Tell what is to happen next, or how you would like the situation resolved.

6. Imagine yourself to be a famous historical character towards the end of your life. Give the essence of this life in a first-person account

7. Using one of the techniques of free association, start from the word ANIMAL. If a useful train of ideas follows, draft a short poem. Try again using MACHINE for another short poem. Could you use ideas from the two lists to write a poem of contrasts? If my subjects don't work, use your own.

8. Using the stream of consciousness technique, write down your thoughts for ten minutes. Put the work away without reading it until next day. Then see if it contains any ideas which you can use as the basis of a poem.

9. Think of a poem you know well, and write down in one sentence what it is about. Draft another poem with a similar theme, but using entirely different incidents and imagery.

(optional)

10. Imagine you have a Muse standing behind you, or a creative helper sitting opposite. Write down whatever is dictated to you. If nothing happens, it doesn't matter, because you already have more than nine poems to work on.

Keep all your drafts. You will be looking back on them as the book progresses.

CHAPTER 2

WORDS

You have the first vague shape of a poem, like a new canvas delivered to a painter, but whereas his medium is expensive, and mistakes dear, your raw materials are free, with second thoughts costing no more than crossing-out.

You must decide early on what kind of words you want. There are thousands, printed everywhere you look, rushing through your ears, snuggled up intimately with thoughts in your brain. A complete poem is more than a string of words of course, but as even a Leonardo portrait is paint on canvas, so poems are sounds in air, or the preserved version on paper. Let's take a quick look at language then, rather in the way a painter considers the potential of paint.

If you are writing in English, you are in one way lucky. At least two and a half languages have gone into making it: Anglo-Saxon and Latin, much of it via Norman French. A worldwide former Empire added travellers' phrase-books in a dozen more. Every colour of expression is yours for the picking. No other language is as rich in synonyms.

In another way you are unlucky for the same reason. With such choice, where do you begin? This may seem like a silly question. Why not simply decide what you want to say, and just let the words come? Given sincerity of feeling, the expression follows naturally. Or does it? Here is an experiment for you to try – in imagination if you prefer. Take a large hammer in one hand, and prepare to drive a nail into a piece of wood. Instead of hitting the nail on the head though, hit your thumb on the nail. Say something spontaneously. Now do you think what you said, quite likely ****! or even ****!! will convey your feelings to others? Will these words enable them to see the black and green bruises? You must somehow create a resonance in the minds of your listeners/readers, making them imagine or remember a similar experience.

You should select words for poetry with three things in mind: meaning, associations and sound, trying to make all three work together for your special purpose.

Meaning

People often read extra significance into poetry where in prose they would be content with one word, one meaning. Because a lot of older poetry is multi-layered, educated readers are conditioned to expect this. Consider this sentence: The cat sat on the mat.

What kind of cat? What kind of mat? Very likely just a household moggie, upright on a hearthrug. In the context you might find them, a child's reading-book, there is often a picture to prove you right. Transfer the cat and mat to a line of verse, however:

The cat clawed at the mat of night.

Is *cat* black, ginger, Persian, Siamese, my lovable Purrkin or the flea-ridden, bird-murdering Catastrophe down the road?

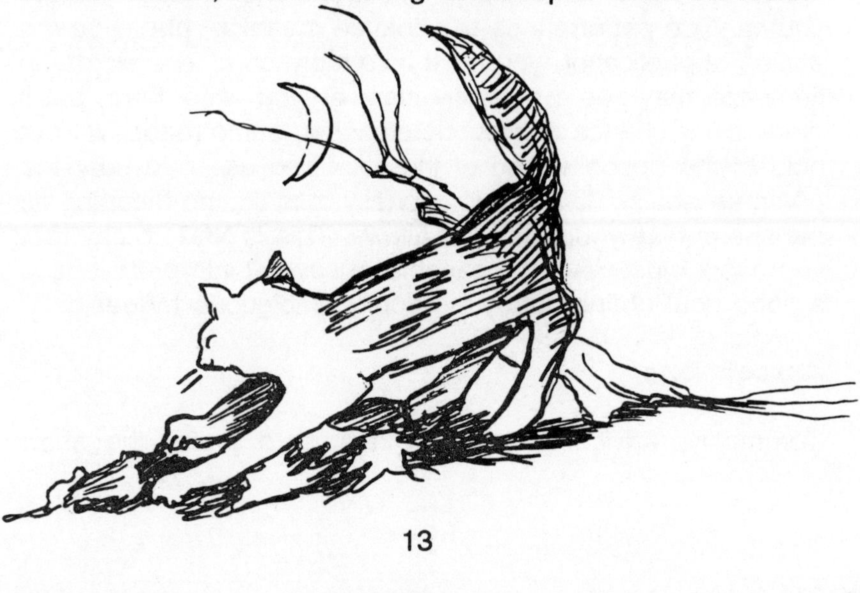

Cat might be tiger of many kinds in zoo or jungle, even tyger, burning bright. *Cat* is spiteful acquaintance, *cat* is cool or fat. Do you want some, or all of the above? Though you wipe your feet on *mat* you may also use it to sleep on or for protection. It could be a tangled mass of something like hair. All such meanings can be exploited, but the words must be controlled to exclude those you don't want. The point is that you must be aware, as you revise your poem, of the different possibilities.

You can qualify or expand if you need to:

The hunting cat clawed at the mat of night.

That makes the type of cat clearer, and the line more menacing, but you may have lost a little energy. The meaning is getting more precise, but the poetry is not necessarily improved. You must make a decision whether to go back to your first version, or, more likely, play around a bit longer. There will be more about this later on.

In speech, there are clues to meaning apart from the words: tone, emphasis, the rise and fall of the tune of the utterance, facial expression and body language generally. Try saying this aloud, first as if you hadn't eaten for two days, then as if you were feeling sick: *I'd love some peaches and cream.*

If you intend to read your poems aloud and never print them you can use performance to reinforce meaning, but if you are aiming at publication you must take more care. The words on the page may seem perfectly clear as you write them, but if there is any chance of misunderstanding, some reader will get hold of the opposite end of the stick and use it to beat the poem senseless. It is simple courtesy to make the meaning as transparent as your intention allows. This is NOT to say that your work must never be capable of several interpretations – a good deal of fine poetry is happily ambiguous by design.

Associations

Commonly, advice given to writers is to prefer the short

Anglo-Saxon word to the multi-syllabled Latin one. The plainer words often have to do with simply staying alive - concerning the body *(bone, heart)* food and drink *(meat, beer)* houses *(room, roof)* and kinship *(mother, child)*. They are often the ones we use most in everyday speech, carrying the elemental charge of life. Use them when you want a blunt, urgent effect. Latin words often concern society, law, religion, medicine and academic disciplines. They can be elegant, subtle, or have an exact scientific meaning.

My advice is merely to become sensitive to differences of language, so that you can choose according to need. If you picked badly, you might produce this kind of thing:

I can proffer no alternative to sanguinary sacrifice, stressful labour, lachrymosity and effort sufficient to cause perspiration.
Which is not at all what Churchill said!

Yet sometimes the long word is the right one:

I wish I had the voice of Homer
To sing of rectal carcinoma.
(J.B.S. Haldane. from 'Cancer's a Funny Thing')

Sometimes, like Macbeth, you may want to make a point twice for emphasis, once in long, once in short words:

No, this my hand will rather
The multitudinous seas incarnadine,
Making the green one red.
(Shakespeare *Macbeth II.i)*

This is having the best of both styles, the short words even more stark by contrast.

Every word and phrase you use will have associations for you and for your reader. You choose them largely because of the load of meanings they carry for you, but you can't know for certain what they conjure up for someone else. However there are also formalised associations that you should be aware of, because these *will* be shared by many of your readers.

For example, you may be a keen gardener, particularly fond

of lilies. For you, *lily* will bring to mind colours, scent, possibly feelings of joy, the recollection of summer. In the public domain, *lily* has symbolic hooks to Christianity and the Virgin, standing for purity, and the lotus lily has a special significance for Buddhists. Also quite commonly lilies are associated with funerals, with grief or loss. But suppose one of your readers once fell over and broke an arm while carrying a bunch? The private association could ruin your careful line. That's simply bad luck.

What you can do is to pay great attention to tone and register and make the most of them. 'Tone' conveys the general atmosphere of a poem: is it formal, conversational, rhetorical, childlike? 'Register' overlaps this, but also refers to the special form of language used by different professions, or in different social circumstances.

For instance, imagine you are a doctor. First, explain to your child's friend why Johnny can't go out to play today: 'Johnny's got something the matter with his throat. It's very sore and he's in bed.'

Now tell his teacher about it: 'Johnny's gone down with tonsillitis. He feels very poorly.'

But this afternoon you have to address your fellow doctors at a conference on the diseases of childhood: 'My own son appears to be suffering from acute streptococcal tonsillitis of abrupt onset, with widespread inflammation of the throat and a moderate degree of constitutional disturbance.'

The information you give on each occasion is more or less the same, but the phrases you choose change according to the people you're speaking to. If you told Johnny's six-year-old friend about 'streptococcal tonsillitis' he wouldn't understand at all, whereas if you got up at the formal conference to say that there was 'something the matter' with your son, they'd hardly be impressed by your professionalism. Some people use different registers even in something as simple as a greeting – 'Good morning' to a distant acquaintance, 'Hello' to the milkman, and possibly 'Hi!' to a friend. Becoming aware of differences in register can help you to convey nuances of meaning in various kinds of poetry.

In historical tides of fashion there is a tendency for poetry to become stylised, sometimes even with a register of its own – poetic diction. This is followed by a revolution, as new poets return to a colloquial register, until this too hardens into a convention and another revolution is required. The Romantics are one example, rebelling against the formality of Pope, Dryden and other Augustans, and using 'a selection of the language really used by men'. The modern movement at the beginning of this century is another, in which the mannerisms of the Georgian poets were thrown out, and several new waves have hit the beach since then.

Iconoclasm is always done with the best intentions – it is a movement towards sincerity and real-life concerns when poetic standards have become too intellectual or rigid.

It must be emphasised though, that there is no 'right' language (or subject) for poetry. The only criterion is: does it express your thought, and does it come off for your audience in a way which has made them see or feel a small part of the world in a new way?

Consider these lines, all effective in their fashion:

Hail, holy Light! offspring of heav'n first-born,
(Milton *Paradise Lost. Book III*)

[He] Cocked up a squint eye and said, 'I bloody
did that.'
(John Ormond, from 'Cathedral Builders')

Whither away, fair rover, and what thy quest?
(Robert Bridges, from 'A Passer-by')

Where are you going to, my pretty maid?
(Nursery Rhyme/Folksong)

The first is a formal invocation. Light is addressed not only as if it were a person, but a divine person, superior even to Christ. There is the Biblical association of 'Let there be light' and the emotional charge of 'first-born' carrying the idea of most beloved. The language is dignified and rhetorical, though at the same time it conveys strong feeling.

By contrast, the second is about a humble craftsman who had helped to build a medieval cathedral. His emotion is as valid as Milton's, but John Ormond uses the register of an inarticulate workman - a modern workman, with the result that the historical distance between then and now is wiped out. You can see his dusty hands.

Robert Bridges' line has the opposite effect. Old-fashioned words like *whither* and *thy* and the mystical *quest* suggest something not quite real, and restrained, intellectualised emotion. It was partly the fashion of his times (1844-1930) to use high-flown diction, but nevertheless for a skilled poet (who also promoted the work of G.M. Hopkins) it must have been a deliberate choice.

Nothing intellectual about the last example. Straight to the point, though with a patronising ring to 'my pretty maid', the young man deserves the snub he's going to get at the end.

Sentence Length

Spoken phrases are limited by the amount of breath available, but the writing hand can take as long as it likes to get to the point - to be long-winded, in fact. Just as colloquial words often sound more sincere than literary ones, so short emotional utterances sound more natural than long ones. And wit, as is well known, demands brevity. But sometimes a long languid sentence may be just what you want - in a poem about an extended siesta, for example.

Compare these, for instance:-

Men!
Two men!
Men! The only animal in the world to fear!
(D.H. Lawrence, from 'Mountain Lion')

The cow is of the bovine ilk;
One end is moo, the other, milk.
(Ogden Nash)

But propt on beds of amaranth and moly,
How sweet (while warm airs lull us, blowing lowly)
With half-dropt eyelid still,
Beneath a heaven dark and holy,
To watch the long bright river drawing slowly
His waters from the purple hill – ...
(Tennyson, from 'The Lotos-Eaters Choric Song')

Freshness

You are using a language already polished by the tongues of millions. Unless you invent another of your own – which no-one else would understand anyhow – you cannot hope to be more than partially original in your use of words. (Original thought and imagery is another matter.) You can perhaps get away with a few new words if you make the meaning clear by context or derivation, but too many irritate readers.

There is a constant walk along a narrow wall between on the one side words that draw their strength from their common associations and normal syntax, and on the other side the poet's desire to give his ideas fresh expression. There are a good many word-groups which, though not quite clichés, are worn bland with use. Take *fluffy white clouds* for instance. Clouds are fluffy and frequently white, but does the phrase excite you? If you catch yourself using obviously associated words, it's worth reconsideration. For instance you might find a simile for the *fluffy white* idea – whipped cream? soapsuds? raw meringues? what else is fluffy and white?

Clichés, often brilliantly expressive metaphors originally, but over-circulated for that very reason, are to be avoided (like the plague!) unless you need them for a deliberate purpose. They carry the negative resonance of banality. Use your own individual speech patterns when you can, as they are your unique voice. And of course, do feel free to use contractions such as *can't* and *won't* to sound natural.

Dialect poems? They can be intriguing and sound authentic, but have the disadvantage of not being as readily understood as those in standard English. That's a decision you must make according to the audience you want to reach and the persona of the poem. You also have to be very thoroughly steeped in the particular dialect you're using to achieve credibility.

Sounds of Words

One could argue that the music of words is more important than their meaning; though the balance between sound and sense will naturally vary from one poet to another.

We'll be looking at this in more detail later on but for the moment please just read aloud and listen to the following:–

But the majestic river floated on
Out of the mist and hum of that low land
Into the frosty starlight, and there moved
Rejoicing, through the hushed Chorasmian waste,
Under the solitary moon.
(Matthew Arnold, from 'Sohrab and Rustum')

The darksome burn, horseback brown,
His rollrock highroad roaring down,
In coop and in comb the fleece of his foam
Flutes and low to the lake falls home.
(Gerard Manley Hopkins, from 'Inversnaid')

And these, which both come from another poem:–

Willows whiten, aspens quiver,
Little breezes dusk and shiver
Thro' the wave that runs for ever
By the island in the river
Flowing down to Camelot.

In the stormy east-wind straining,
The pale yellow woods were waning,

The broad stream in his bank complaining,
Heavily the low sky raining
Over tower'd Camelot ...
(Tennyson, from 'The Lady of Shalott')

All these quotations have to do with the flow of water in river or stream, and all incidentally are by Victorian poets, craft-masters, but you might like to consider the following questions, to help clarify the different effects they produce.

- Which is the quickest-flowing water?
- Which carries the greatest volume of water?
- How do you know this? Are there clues from sound or meaning or both?
- Which one would you prefer to go boating on?
- In what kind of boat?
- Do any of them represent a threat?
- How do you respond to each quotation emotionally?
- Do you think that the rhythm has anything to do with your feeling? If so, what?
- Can you separate your responses to the sounds of the words and to their meaning?
- What differences in the sounds can you discover between the first and second quotations from Tennyson?

PRACTICE WRITING

1. To become aware of different registers, pick three poems from a modern anthology and look at the kind of language used. What registers were chosen? Are the poems formal, colloquial, slangy? Do they use technical language? Do they differ from each other, and are they consistent in each poem? Do you think the general tone suits the subject-matter in each case? Try rewriting one of these, using a different register e.g. a love poem in medical jargon, or as it might be written formally by a civil servant. Notice the potential for comedy/satire if the wrong register is used deliberately.

2. Find out what registers are natural for you in different circumstances. For instance, for the register of *complaint*, write a letter

(in prose) about a delay on a train-journey, or a defective pair of shoes. Using some of the same vocabulary of complaint, write a poem expressing frustration about a physical handicap or loss of something/someone dear to you. Does it work? If not, what changes would you make? E.g. do you need a *more* or *less* formal tone?

3. Write three short poems to include word-and-sound pictures of the following: a hurricane which caused damage to trees and houses; traffic on a busy street, including a juggernaut and a bicycle; an empty house, silent except for a dripping tap and the sound of your own footsteps and breathing.

4. Now go back to the drafts of the first three poems you wrote after reading Chapter 1. Look at the register you used in each case. There may not be much difference, but I'd expect the first to be more Anglo-Saxon and colloquial than the last, with the second between the two. Would they be improved by making any changes in the levels of language between everyday speech and formality? (N.B. I'm only asking. You can say NO if you want to!)

5. Look at the draft poem about the historical character. Is it written as if you were living today, or did you include some words and phrases to give it a period flavour? If not, would the poem gain anything by using them? If so, would the poem lose much by leaving them out? Write both versions and compare them.

6. (a) Open any good dictionary at random and start to look at the words. Take the first five that you often use in conversation. Have these words any further or compound meanings that you were not aware of? If so, start a list in your notebook (the one you bought during Chapter One).
(b) Take the first five nouns. Would any of these words be suitable for use as the title of a poem? Start a separate list of these. Draft the poems too, by all means.
(c) Would any be unsuitable? If so, why? Repeat this exercise as often as you like. Another way of putting it: begin to collect words that might come in useful, and polish the ones you own already.

CHAPTER 3

PATTERNS OF RHYTHM

Rhythm is a part of being alive. Think of the in-and-out of breathing, the left-right of walking and the beat of a heart first heard in the womb. Ordinary speech itself has rhythm, caused by the stress-patterns of the language, which must be influenced by the amount of breath in an average pair of lungs.

Rhythm is inherent in physical work: chopping wood, grinding corn, digging, knitting, kneading bread. Rhythms abound in nature, though they are not necessarily regular: wind in trees, waves on the shore, the dawn chorus of birds, rain on the roof. Nowadays too, the rhythm of machinery impinges on everyone. Anything containing a motor or wheels is certain to have a regular rhythm. Remember for a moment the sound of a car engine; of a tractor; of a train; of a washing-machine.

To seem alive, to mesh into the processes of thought and feeling, poetry too must have rhythm. Prose has it as well, of course, but poetry, because it is closer to the heart of things, needs to have a more obviously recognisable pulse.

In fact a physical pulse is a good example of a rhythm which can be transferred to verse. Do you suppose there could be a connection between the lub-dup of a steady heart, and the ti-tum of an iambic foot in verse? In any case, just as the mother's heartbeat soothes the unborn baby, so a very regular rhythm is reassuring - and if too monotonous can send the hearer to sleep. This is what you want if you are singing a lullaby and rocking a cradle, but probably not otherwise. The effect of regular rhythm is slightly hypnotic, or at least engages the right, artistic hemisphere of the brain.

A strong rhythm also arouses emotion, a fact as well known to orators as to successful poets. Marching songs once kept up the courage of soldiers going to the wars, and sea-shanties helped a group of people literally to pull together as a team.

Notice in these last two examples that the sounds of music, the sense of the words and the rhythms of both are all stirred together to produce a song. Poetry has a strong affinity with music – lyric poetry was originally poetry accompanied by plucking a lyre, and the words for popular songs are still called 'lyrics'.

It can be helpful to consider poetry as being like music, or maybe halfway between music and meaning. I said in the last chapter it is important to choose a register appropriate for subject and mood. Now I suggest it's just as important to choose a suitable rhythm. Consider the tone of your writing. Is it a happy, brisk allegro, or a mournful adagio? Would it be appropriate to write in a lively way, con brio? Do you want your effects piano, or forte? Some poets have even used the names of musical compositions as titles – *Aubade* and *Four Quartets* for instance, and the tone and rhythm follow accordingly.

Useful Metres

In traditional metrical verse the basic unit is a *foot,* a group of syllables. A syllable is a word or part of a word which you can say by itself, if you want to: *A fine day* (3 syllables); *A per–fect day* (4 syllables); *A tru–ly mag–ni–fi–cent day* (8 syllables). A foot in verse corresponds roughly to a musical bar. The feet are ranged into lines, the lines into *stanzas* or verses, often in a scheme which is repeated again and again.

Metre is not the same as rhythm – rhythm is organic, and though the word implies a pattern, this need not be absolutely regular, as metre is. Metre can be measured in steady beats, just as music can be 'kept in time' with a metronome.

Poets writing in a traditional way need to have the orthodox metres at their finger–tips (literally, counting the beats). The names are copied from classical models, because the scholars who named them had great respect for Latin and Greek poet–

ry, and tried to make similar rules apply to English, though the languages differ too much for this to be entirely satisfactory.

However, the system is based on the simple observation that in English speech some syllables are more stressed than others: a MUG of TEA; CHEERful PEOple; CULpable HOMicide. You can make an abstract pattern: if ti=unstressed, tum=stressed, then these examples are ti–tum ti–tum; tum–ti tum–ti; and tum–ti–ti tum–ti–ti. For convenience, the symbols ⏑(unstressed) and –(stressed) are often used.

MUG OF TEA
CHEERFUL PEOPLE
CULPABLE HOMICIDE

Iambic meter

The ⏑ –(ti–tum) metre is *iambic*, pronounced 'I am bick'. A single foot is an iamb (old-fashioned name, iambus).

When writing in any metre, you must first let your reader get used to it. For example, take the first stanza of 'La Belle Dame Sans Merci' by Keats, which starts:

˘ ¯ ˘ ¯ ˘ ¯ ˘ ¯
Oh what / can ail/ thee, knight/-at-arms

A whole poem written like this would be very dull though, and besides, too difficult to write, because language doesn't jerk along like a machine. The real skill in this kind of poetry is in playing off, or counterpointing, the expected, metronome-like stresses of metre with the rhythm of what is actually said.

Even in this first line there's a pause in the middle of a foot, between *thee* and *knight*. After this, words themselves start to insist on variety:

˘ ¯ ˘ ¯ ˘ ¯ ˘ ˘
Alone/ and pale/ly loit/ering,

You wouldn't say 'LOITerING', would you?
Then back to the basic metre:

˘ ¯ ˘ ¯ ˘ ¯ ˘ ¯
The sedge/ has with/ered from/ the lake,

followed by something new:

˘ ¯ ¯ ¯
And no/ birds/ sing.

A shorter line, three feet, not four. That is often done. But the last two feet have been varied by leaving out unstressed syll-ables. Suppose Keats had written:

˘ ¯ ˘ ¯ ˘ ¯
And not/ a bird/ will sing.

Would this have a different effect?

All sorts of variations are possible, once you have signalled your standard metre. A very common way is to reverse the foot, to put a trochee (see below) where an iamb is expected, or to add or subtract a syllable. What is happening here?:

That's my last Duchess painted on the wall,
Looking as if she were alive. I call
That piece a wonder now: Fra Pandolf's hands
Worked busily a day, and there she stands.
(Robert Browning, from 'My Last Duchess')

Can you hear the natural rhythm of speech overlying but not cancelling out the basic iambic metre?

The danger is that if you alter too many feet, the original beat gets forgotten, and it may sound as if you don't know what you're doing. Your ear is your best friend. Read your poems aloud to yourself or to a tape recorder. Ask yourself: have I made the metre strong enough to be felt in the background? Have I varied the actual stress-patterns to give surprise and excitement, and to sound natural? - In other words, is the poem rhythmical, but not boring?

Blank verse

One of the most important manifestations of iambic metre has five feet to the line - *iambic pentameter.* It is used for *blank verse,* 'blank' because it doesn't rhyme. And for this reason it is flexible, suitable for long poems and drama. The line is long enough to vary some feet without the basic metre lapsing, letting the natural breaks and pauses of speech occur at different positions, avoiding monotony. Often you must read the sentence as a whole, continuing past the end of the line into the next. Its different treatments can be seen by comparing these extracts, both having to do with hallucinations:

Is this a dagger that I see before me,
The handle toward my hand? Come, let me clutch thee:-
I have thee not, and yet I see thee still.
Art thou not, fatal vision, sensible
To feeling as to sight? Or art thou but
A dagger of the mind, a false creation
Proceeding from the heat-oppressed brain?
(Shakespeare, from *Macbeth* Act II Sc.1)

... my boat
Went heaving through the water like a swan;
When, from behind that craggy steep till then
The horizon's bound, a huge peak, black and huge,
As if with voluntary power instinct
Upreared its head. I struck and struck again,
And growing still in stature the grim shape
Towered up between me and the stars ...
(Wordsworth, from *The Prelude*)

Iambic metre is the one that fits English best, and is most common, but there are many others. The complete list is long so let's keep to essentials – too many feet can trip you up.

Trochaic metre

A *trochee* is the reverse of an iamb:- tum–ti instead of ti–tum. (Trochee is pronounced to rhyme with 'smoky', and is an example of itself.) But poems in sustained trochaic metre are comparatively few – the longest one I can think of is Longfellow's *Hiawatha:*

– ◡ – ◡ – ◡ – ◡
Swift of/ foot was/ Hia/watha;
He could shoot an arrow from him,
And run forward with such fleetness,
That the arrow fell behind him!

If the trochees are regular, the lines must end with unstressed syllables. For a stronger effect, the unstressed half can be left out, ending on the stressed syllable:

– ◡ – ◡ – ◡ –
Tiger!/ Tiger!/ burning/ bright
In the forests of the night,
What immortal hand or eye
Could frame thy fearful symmetry?
(William Blake, from 'The Tiger')

As before, some of the feet are reversed. The last line could be considered iambic, though it depends on the way it's said.

Anapaestic metre

An *anapaest* (pronounced 'annapest') is a foot of three syllables: ti–ti–tum, ˘˘–.

> ˘ ˘ – ˘ – ˘ ˘ – ˘ ˘ –
> *Not a drum/ was heard,/ not a fun/eral note,*
>
> ˘ ˘ – ˘ ˘ – ˘ ˘ – ˘
> *As his corse/ to the ram/part we hurr/ied;*
> *Not a soldier discharged his farewell shot*
> *O'er the grave where our hero we buried.*
> (Charles Wolfe from 'The Burial of Sir John Moore..')

This metre is even more difficult to keep up for long – in this short example, several feet are irregular. Nevertheless, you can feel its ghostly knocking in counterpoint with the actual stresses.

Dactylic metre

The fourth important foot is a Greek finger! A *dactyl,* tum–ti–ti, –˘˘, like the three bones of a skeleton finger. (Same word is part of the dinosaur pterodactyl.) Like the anapaest, it is seldom found in long stretches, but mixes with other feet. This example includes the *spondee* with two (almost) equal stresses:

> – ˘ ˘ – – – ˘ ˘ –
> *Lonely the/ sea–bird/ lies at her/rest,*
>
> – ˘ ˘ – – – ˘ ˘ –
> *Blown like a/ dawn–blenched/ parcel of/ spray*
>
> ˘ – ˘ – ˘ – ˘ ˘ –
> *Upon the/ wind, or/ follows her/ prey*
>
> – ˘ ˘ – – – ˘ ˘ –
> *Under a/ great wave's/ hollowing/ crest.*
> (W.B. Yeats from 'Lonely the sea–bird...')

Falling and rising rhythm

Falling rhythm is one which is mostly trochaic or dactylic, the stress occurring on the first syllable of the foot. Some people think that it gives a more melancholy tone than the opposite, rising rhythm. The latter is iambic or anapaestic, with the stress on the last syllable. A falling rhythm does perhaps suggest fading out, but it also depends a great deal on other factors whether your verse seems happy or sad.

Length of metrical lines

A line can have any number of feet from one (very uncommon) to six or even seven (very, very uncommon). The favourite numbers are three, four and five, as with ballad meter and iambic pentameter. Shorter lines, as you might expect, have a quicker movement, suitable for action-poems, while longer lines lend themselves to descriptive kinds of verse. There will be more about line-lengths and forms in the next chapter.

Pauses

Conventional poetry relies on ordinary punctuation to mark a pause, there being no widely-accepted 'rest' symbol as there is in music. Of course there is long pause between one stanza and the next, and a slight hesitation at a line end. But an interesting pause occurs very often in the middle of a line. This is the *caesura.* A skilful poet varies its position to avoid monotony:

> *Surprised by joy – // impatient as the Wind*
> *I turned to share the transport – // O! with whom*
> *But Thee, // deep buried in the silent tomb,*
> *That spot which no vicissitude can find.*
> (Wordsworth, from 'Desideria')

Modern poets have greater flexibility, leaving gaps within or between lines if they want to, as part of an experimental approach to lay-out:

> *As the rain falls*
> *so does*

your love
bathe every
open
object of the world –
(William Carlos Williams, from 'Rain')

Free verse

I have said that, historically, when poetic diction becomes too conventional, younger poets throw it out and use language in a different way. This also happened to French traditional forms and metres at the end of the nineteenth century.

A group of poets, including Rimbaud and Verlaine, wrote with a strong emphasis on imagery and symbols, with the aim of getting closer to the way the mind actually works. Regular metres seemed too artificial, and in their place they put the cadences of 'vers libre', verse freed from the prison of metre. NOT free from rhythm, please note, and their use of 'cadence' emphasises the kinship between poetry and music.

It was not entirely a new idea. Walt Whitman had already done something of the same kind in America. You could argue that the translators of the Bible did so too. G.M. Hopkins was writing some poems in 'sprung rhythm' also towards the end of the century, though his work was not published until later. In this, the stresses of speech dictate the rhythm, unstressed syllables don't count, and there is no counterpointing of metre and speech pattern. Several strongly stressed words can follow each other closely:

I am all at once what Christ is, since he was what I am, and
This Jack, joke, poor potsherd, patch, matchwood, immortal diamond,
Is immortal diamond.
(From 'That Nature is a Heraclitean Fire and of the comfort of the Resurrection')

But an even freer free verse was certainly publicised by the Symbolists. After it was taken up by poets as gifted as W.B.

Yeats and T.S. Eliot it became a fashionable way to write in English and remains so.

At its best, free verse is as moving, as much 'poetry' as anything written in the past. At its worst it sounds like prose, sometimes good, sometimes bad prose, sliced up so as to waste paper with unnecessarily wide margins. It is more difficult to write good free verse than to write acceptable traditional verse, where at least the scaffolding of the rules supports the building.

Bad free verse is responsible, I think, for some of the loss of public respect which poetry has suffered in this century. If all you need are a few startling phrases slapped down in irregular lines, no need to bother about rhythm or form, no wonder some people find the results disappointing.

If you write in free verse, cadences - speech rhythms, more or less formalised - must be very carefully worked out. Additional devices such as alliteration, repetition, pauses and other of the 'secret patterns' to be described later, are even more necessary than in traditional poetry. Take this for instance:

We do not wish anything to happen.
Seven years we have lived quietly,
Succeeded in avoiding notice,
Living and partly living.
There have been oppression and luxury,
There have been poverty and licence,
There has been minor injustice.
Yet we have gone on living,
Living and partly living.

(T.S. Eliot, from *Murder in the Cathedral*)

There are a number of patterns here. Firstly, there are three or four main stressed syllables in each line. Each line ends with an unstressed syllable. There are several repetitions - the obvious one of a whole line given twice, but also the pattern of 'there have been ...' and the balancing opposites of *oppression/luxury, poverty/licence*. Listen to all those 'p' and 'l' sounds too.

Good free verse of this kind is attractive in an anti-heroic age like ours. The rhythm of ordinary speech tricks the hearer into thinking it *is* ordinary speech, unrehearsed and sincere – though Eliot may have worked for hours to make it sound so.

'Listen, now, verse should be as natural
As the small tuber that feeds on muck
And grows slowly from obtuse soil
To the white flower of immortal beauty.'

'Natural, hell! What was it Chaucer
Said once about the long toil
That goes like blood to the poem's making?'
(R.S. Thomas from 'Poetry for Supper')

Free verse has brought everyday realism into the poem's space, where it is recreated as something extraordinary:

She was buckets
and water flouncing into them.
She was winds pouring wetly
round house-ends.
She was brown eggs, black skirts
and a keeper of threepennybits
in a teapot.
(From 'Aunt Julia' by Norman MacCaig)

Syllabic verse

An interesting compromise between free and traditional verse is found in syllabics, imported from Japan or borrowed from some Welsh forms. Here, instead of a pattern of poetic feet, there is a rigid count of syllables, with stresses falling wherever convenient, and rhymed or not, as you like. For instance, the Japanese *haiku* is well known. It is a very short unrhymed poem of three lines, with 5, 7 and 5 syllables in each:

This long recession:
At the end of my tee-square
A spider starts work.
(Brian Cater)

The Welsh *englyn* is something similar. There are variations, but a usual form has four lines, of ten, six, seven and seven syllables. The end words of lines 2, 3 and 4 rhyme with the sixth syllable of the first line. It sounds complicated, but is not.

CITY NOCTURNE

Clouds and moon dance, in white on a black drop,
silent ballets of night;
instead of music the bright
low windows of human light.
(Katherine Knight)

In plain syllabic verse your lines can be of any length, and they need not all be the same, but the pattern should be repeated exactly in each stanza. Marianne Moore is a well-known exponent of the system. On the page it has the shape of poetry, but is apt to sound like prose.

Accentual verse

Instead of seeking new rhythms, would you prefer to be oldfangled, going back to the beginnings of English, to adapt or borrow something of this venerable system? An Anglo-Saxon line of poetry had a regular number of stressed syllables, never mind the unstressed ones. There was a strongly-marked caesura in the middle, and at least three out of four of the stressed syllables alliterated. (That is, they began with the same sound. More about alliteration in Chapter Nine.)

Langland used this pattern in *Piers Plowman* in the fourteenth century:

In a somer seson   whan soft was the sonne
I shope me in shroudes   as I a shepe were,

In habit as an heremite   unholy of workes,
Went wyde in this world   wondres to here

Words without rhythm of some sort can never be poetry. But in working out which system is best for whatever you are writing at present, remember that poetry came before 'rules of versification', which tried to describe what had already happened. Many, if not most poets find them useful sometimes as guidelines, but the only really unbreakable law is to satisfy the mind's ear and the heart's measure.

PRACTICAL WORK

1. Write down a stanza of a traditional poem that you like. Go through it, marking the stressed and unstressed syllables with – or ⌣. What kind of verse is used? Iambic, trochaic, anapestic or dactylic? Is it perfectly regular, or are some feet different from the basic metre?

2. Find examples if you can of the other three kinds. What difference in mood can you detect between all these poems? How much does this depend on the rhythm, how much on the subject, how much on the verbal register? Which metres make the lines move quickly, which slowly?

3. Has any of your previous work got a metrical pattern? If so, would the poem be improved by making it a) more or b) less regular? Try out both ways.

4. Have another look at your ANIMAL and MACHINE poem. Was the rhythm/metre different in each section? Try another contrasting pair, using free verse for a poem about a specific animal, such as an elephant, traditional metre for one about a car or train. (Think about W.H.Auden's *Night Mail* that begins:

   This is the Night Mail crossing the Border,
   Bringing the cheque and the postal order.)

5. (Easy) Write a poem about a ticking clock, using its sound to set the rhythm. (It might run down, or someone

might wind it up.)
(More difficult) Write two short contrasting poems titled LEGATO and STACCATO. They may or may not be about music, but make the rhythms appropriate to each, whether you use a traditional metre or otherwise. Also consider the length of lines – the second poem might have shorter lines than the first.

6. Speech rhythms: tape a short extract from a conversation or radio programme and write down a few sentences. Go through it marking it as in 1 above. Do any patterns strike you? If so, could you use one or more as the basic rhythm(s) of a new poem? Repeat this exercise as often as you like.

7. Choose a word of power (page 7), and using a free association technique draft a few ideas. Write several natural–sounding sentences using the first two or three. Break the sentences into lines to make a stanza, count the syllables and finish the poem in the same syllabic pattern.

8. Invent a rhythm that you can clap, using a mixture of different feet until you find one that pleases you. Write it down in the ⏑ – notation. Allow words to suggest themselves in this pattern. An insistent rhythm can be a starting point for a poem as much as an insistent idea.

CHAPTER 4

PATTERNS OF RHYME AND OTHER REPETITIONS

Rhyming is fun. Very young children appreciate it as part of the joy of language. Yet serious poetry can be written perfectly well, maybe even better, without it. If Shakespeare, Milton and Wordsworth could dispense with rhyme in their best work, so can you. But on the other hand, if Chaucer, Byron, Tennyson, – and Shakespeare, Milton and Wordsworth – could use it with delight, so, too, can you.

Full rhyme

If a word happens to have nearly the same sound as another, it's interesting. It signals 'Listen for the next!' Full rhyme is easily recognised: the same end-sound of stressed syllables, such as *beat, cheat, entreat, feet, complete, street...* For hundreds of years it has been a main ingredient of verse (though not necessarily of poetry, as I said). As well as its inherent musicality, rhyming is a way of drawing attention to metrical patterns. This is particularly so when lines are of different lengths. Because the rhyme signals the end of the line, you can't mistake it:

The glories of our blood and state
Are shadows, not substantial things;
There is no armour against Fate;
Death lays his icy hand on kings;
Sceptre and Crown
Must tumble down,
And in the dust be equal made
With the poor crooked scythe and spade.
(James Shirley, from 'Death the Leveller')

If the line end is also the end of a sentence or clause, needing a punctuation mark, the thump is even more noticeable. It is an *end-stopped* line. A skilful craftsman therefore plays off the sentence against the line structure, often avoiding the need to draw breath at the rhyme. In the above, for instance, the grammatical unit is 'The glories of our blood and state are shadows.' This running-on of sense between lines is called *enjambment.* Too much of it, however, results in the ear losing the pattern, so you need a well-judged mixture of end-stopped and enjambed lines.

Rhyme is also a useful device to link ideas or images together, and to bring a thought, sentence or stanza to a satisfying finish. Shakespeare very often used a rhymed couplet to sign off a scene, like the falling of a verbal curtain.

If well done, not overdone, it gives an impression of elegance. Because it suggests having the last word, it is useful for light verse where wit is needed. Consider this:

WINE, WOMEN AND WEDDING

The glances over cocktails
That seemed to be so sweet
Don't seem quite so amorous
Over the Shredded Wheat.
(Anon.)

Would 'cornflakes' do instead? Some verse depends entirely for its effect on unusual or ingenious rhyming:

COMMON MARKETEER

He left his native land to mock and stare
At not-quite-us and funny foreign ways,
But came back like a pilgrim, full of praise,
An eager convert to their Camembert.
(Katherine Knight)

Placing of rhyme-words

End-rhymes are the most common, but other placings are possible. There are modern examples of initial rhymes - Edith Sitwell has a few - but the principle goes back at least as far as the French poet Pierre de Ronsard (1524?-1585). Here's the first stanza of his poem 'A Cassandre', with rhymes at both beginning and end of the lines:

Mignonne, allons voir si la Rose
Qui ce matin avoit desclose
Sa robe de pourpre au Soleil,
A point perdu ceste vespree
Les plis de sa robe pourpree,
Et son teint au vostre pareil.

[My sweet, let's go and see if the rose, which (only) this morning was showing off its crimson dress to the Sun, hasn't by this evening lost its crimson folds, and complexion which equals your own.]

This poem, incidentally, was the inspiration for Herrick's 'Gather ye rosebuds...' (page 40)

An *internal rhyme* occurs when a word in the middle of a line rhymes with the one at the end. It seems to break a longer unit into two short ones:

In a garden shady this holy lady
With reverent cadence and subtle psalm,
Like a black swan as death came on
Poured forth her song in perfect calm."
(W.H. Auden, from 'Anthem for St Cecilia's Day')

Verse forms with rhyme

Putting rhymes in odd places is a game, entertaining and challenging to try, but nothing like as useful to the poet as end-rhymes, which link lines together by a kind of sympathetic magic:

What is this life if, full of care, rhyme a
We have no time to stand and stare – rhyme a
No time to stand beneath the boughs rhyme b
And stare as long as sheep or cows... rhyme b
(W.H. Davies, from 'Leisure')

These pairs are *couplets.* If you prefer you can have alternate rhyming lines in a four-line *quatrain:*

Gather ye rosebuds while ye may, a
Old Time is still a-flying: b
And this same flower that smiles today a
Tomorrow will be dying. b
(Robert Herrick, 'To the Virgins, to make much of Time')

As a kind of shortspeak, you can say this rhymes *abab.* Then go on through the alphabet with each new rhyme, *cdcd, efef,* etc. For a longer stanza, you might combine the *abab* quatrain with a couplet, *cc.*

I wander'd lonely as a cloud
That floats on high o'er vales and hills,
When all at once I saw a crowd,
A host, of golden daffodils;
Beside the lake, beneath the trees,
Fluttering and dancing in the breeze.
(Wordsworth, from 'Daffodils')

Or perhaps rhymes in general strike your ear as too many? Too obvious? Is it too difficult to find a rhyming word that says what you mean? Economise, but still keep some of rhyme's virtues. Have lines that don't rhyme mixed alternately with those that do:

There lived a wife at Usher's well, a
And a wealthy wife was she; b
She had three stout and stalwart sons, c
And sent them o'er the sea. b
(Traditional, anon. from 'The Wife at Usher's Well')

This is iambic *ballad metre,* lines of four feet alternating with three. The form invites a tune to go with it, and many ballads were originally sung. It is used for hymns and carols too, 'There is a green hill far away' for instance. The simple strong rhythm and rhyme make it easy to remember, suitable for the stories that were handed on from grandparents to children long before TV. The short lines encourage getting to the point, and so move quickly.

This form is flexible enough to use for other poems as well as true ballads:

O my Luve's like a red, red rose
That's newly sprung in June:
O my Luve's like the melodie
That's sweetly play'd in tune.
(Robert Burns from 'A Red, Red Rose')

Another scheme which knits a long poem together is *terza rima,* triplets which rhyme *aba, bcb, cdc, ded* and so on. It has the effect of linking the lines together very smoothly, and is therefore suitable for long narrative poems. It was used by Dante Alighieri in *The Divine Comedy,* and frequently by his translators. Here Dante and his guide, the spirit of Virgil, have just gone through the gates of Hell together:

...I saw folk by a mighty river's side:
Wherefore I said, 'Master, I pray thee let
Me know who these are, by what custom tied,
That makes them seem so ready to pass o'er,
As through the dusky light I have descried.'
Then he:– 'These things shall be accounted for
At the same time that we our footsteps rest
On Acheron's so melancholy shore.'
Then with mine eyes ashamed and downward cast,
Fearing my speech might irksome to him seem,
Far as the river I from parlance ceased.

And lo! towards us in a ship there came
An old man grey with hair of antique mien...
(from *A Vision of Hell: the Inferno of Dante.* translated into English by Charles Tomlinson, 1877)

As a stanza can have any reasonable number of lines – certainly up to eight or nine – many patterns of rhyme are possible. For instance you might have a seven-liner, rhyming *abaa, abb;* or *abc, abc, a;* or *abcc, ded;* or... You can also vary the length of lines in a repeated pattern. Here is an example, *aabccb, ddeffe,* with a rhythm which you can work out for yourself:

You are the town and We are the clock.
We are the guardians of the gate in the rock,
The Two.
On your left and on your right,
In the day and in the night,
We are watching you.

Wiser not to ask just what has occurred
To them who disobeyed our word;
To those
We were the whirlpool, we were the reef,
We were the formal nightmare, grief
And the unlucky rose.
(W.H. Auden and Christopher Isherwood, from a Chorus from *The Dog Beneath the Skin*)

A repetition of a stanza form is itself a large-scale rhythm, contributing a great deal to the overall effect.

Double rhymes

Did you notice in the Herrick quatrain above that both syllables of *flying* rhyme with both syllables of *dying*? Double ones like this are called *feminine rhymes,* – don't ask me why. Be careful with them, unless you are writing comic verse:

Twang the cheeful lute and zither!
Spring is absolutely hither!
Yester eve was dark despair,
With Winter, Winter, everywhere:
Today, upon the other hand,
'Tis Spring throughout this happy land.
Oh, such is Nature's chiaroscuro,
According to the Weather Bureau."
(Ogden Nash, from 'Spring Song')

Repetitions

Not rhymes, but having a similar cyclic effect, are phrases or lines which are repeated without change, or with small changes. A *chorus* or *refrain* is a common feature of many songs, for instance, like this one:

A north-country maid up to London had stray'd
Although with her nature it did not agree;
She wept, and she sigh'd, and she bitterly cried,
`I wish once again in the north I could be.'

(refrain) Oh! the oak, and the ash, and the bonny ivy tree,
They flourish at home in my own country.
(Traditional, from *Oh! the oak and the ash.* 17th Century)

This is repeated after each verse, and brings the song to an end.

You can try for subtle and charming results, as a very old poet did:

He cam all so stille
There his moder was,
As dew in Aprille
That falleth on the grass.

He cam all so stille
To his moderes bowr,
As dew in Aprille,
That falleth on the flowr.
(Anon. from *I sing of a maiden*, 15th century)

Some poems depend on repetition. A *villanelle* for instance, has nineteen lines, only two rhymes, and repeats two of its lines four times each. Read Dylan Thomas's 'Do not go gentle into that good night' for a splendid modern example. It is essential to choose words which are easy to rhyme, of course, such as Thomas's *night* and *day.*

There are other repetitious forms, mostly French, which, like the villanelle, have been copied by writers in English. For instance there are the *rondeau* and *ballade* (not the same as ballad). These are for a virtuoso poet in showing-off mode. Look them up in another book (please see `Books for Poets', p.136) when you have come to the end of this one.

In fact the traditional named forms of poems and stanzas run into many dozens. They are well worth studying. But start with the basic ones, and add to your repertoire gently. As you read poetry, notice what form it takes, and try to estimate how much this adds to the whole effect. Prosody is very interesting once you are interested in prosody! I'll just describe one other important form here: short, with easily grasped rules, and as challenging to write as any poet could want.

The Sonnet

The traditional *sonnet* is a poem of 14 iambic pentameter lines (five feet per line, remember). By convention, its subject is a single thought or feeling. The first eight lines present the theme, which is answered or expanded in the last six. It can be printed without a break, or as eight and six lines, or as three quatrains and a couplet. The rhyme scheme varies. It was an Italian invention, and because Italian has a lot of rhyming words, repeating a rhyme-sound was comparatively easy: *abba, abba, cde, cde.* A variant is *abba, abba, cdcdcd.* Shakespeare made it more flexible: *abab, cdcd, efef, gg.* Other arrangements of the last six lines are allowed.

You can easily find older sonnets in any good traditional anthology, so here's a comparatively recent one, looking at Greek Zeus's rape of Leda in modern terms. Watch the rhyming as well as the rhythms to see how it works:-

LEDA AND THE SWAN

A sudden blow: the great wings beating still a
Above the staggering girl, her thighs caressed b
By the dark webs, her nape caught in his bill, a
Her holds her hapless breast upon his breast. b

How can those terrified vague fingers push c
The feathered glory from her loosening thighs? d
And how can body, laid in that white rush, (c)
But feel the strange heart beating where it lies? d

A shudder in the loins engenders there e
The broken wall, the burning roof and tower f
And Agamemnon dead.
Being so caught up, g
So mastered by the brute blood of the air e
Did she put on his knowledge with his power f
Before the indifferent beak could let her drop? (g)

(W.B.Yeats)

Disadvantages of full rhyme

Although there are a lot of words in English that will rhyme, the commonest ones have been so much exploited over the last six hundred years that many poets feel the system has been exhausted. Stale rhymes have the effect of clichés.

There are dangers, too, in striving after rhymes. First, the need for a particular sound can distort what you want to express. If the exact word you require doesn't rhyme, what are you going to do? Use an inexact word? Or change the previous rhyme? The latter is probably the better option, and a rhyming dictionary can be a great help. But perhaps now the new word slides away from the first meaning. After an evening spent with an overflowing bin, there is a temptation around midnight to make do with an outlandish or archaic word – one which your reader will immediately realise was only put there for the sake of rhyme.

Secondly, it may lead you into the practice of *inversion,* that is altering the natural word-order, to fit in a rhyme word: Shelley's 'Spirit fierce', for instance, instead of 'fierce Spirit', or Yeats' 'shadows deep' to rhyme with 'sleep'. This practice was acceptable in the past, but because it sounds contrived it is much better avoided now.

Thirdly, some people find full rhymes are too obvious, and prefer more sophisticated music.

Near rhyme or half-rhyme

In order to keep some of the advantages of rhyme, modern poets are exploring other correspondences in language. There are many kinds of chiming or similarities that can be used. Don't be put off by the names - which I'll keep to a minimum - but just grasp the principle that sounds which are alike in some way can be put in place of full rhyme.

First there's *light rhyme* where a stressed sound rhymes with an unstressed one: *ring/morning, you/virtue, press/ peerless.*

He walked that room and issued thence
In Galilean turbulence

(Yeats, from 'Two Songs for a Play')

Two unstressed syllables may come together in a very faint echo:

... as when the young bird-catcher
Swept off his tall hat to the Squire's own daughter.

(Robert Graves, from 'Love without Hope')

Pararhyme is close to full rhyme. The last two consonantal sounds of the chiming words are the same, but the vowels are different, as *raid/rode/red/rid/deride/rude, endure/dear/dire, fool/fail/fuel/feel/file* and also *gleam/gloom, trim/tram, brat/brute* and so on.

Consonance simply repeats the last consonantal sound, as *stone/bun/can/broken* or *repeat/cart/shoot.* This is a quiet device, and obviously gives the poet much greater scope because huge numbers of words are available to choose from.

There is, similarly, *assonance* where the vowel-sound is the same, but the consonants are different: *date/made, treat/kneel, bright/crime.*

In the sonnet above you may have noticed the pairs *c (c), push/rush* and *g (g) up/drop.* These are examples of consonance. If you're interested in phonetics you can go into this much more deeply, but for the moment see what you can discover for yourself about these echoes as you read. More in Chapter Nine, too.

It isn't as if all this is completely new. Great poets in the past got away with it, especially when the spelling was the same but the sound different – they called this an *eye rhyme.* Look at this, where (a) and (a) echo, b and b are consonantal rhymes:–

Oh rose, thou art sick! *(a)*
The invisible worm *b*
That flies in the night, *(a)*
In the howling storm ... *b*
(Blake, from 'The Sick Rose')

Here is the beginning of a poem written in regular iambic couplets, but using pararhyme:

It seemed that out of battle I escaped
Down some profound dull tunnel, long since scooped
Through granites which titanic wars had groined.
Yet also there encumbered sleepers groaned,
Too fast in thought or death to be bestirred.
Then, as I probed them, one sprang up, and stared ...
(Wilfred Owen, from 'Strange Meeting')

Here, one using assonance:

I feel the very earth is against me.
Night after night she turns in my sleep
And litters my fields with stones.

I lie out all summer spread like a coat
Over the earth one night after another
Waiting to catch her. ...
(Jeffrey Wainwright, from 'Thomas Müntzer III')

And here the first three stanzas of a poem using a whole fireworks display, including a regular stanzaic pattern, repetition, and near-rhyme, some double. Notice the sequence of *trees/rose/streams/veins/wind/man/lime,* where consonance and assonance give way to echoes, but are still enough to hold the ear. R = a repeated phrase.

The force that through the green fuse drives the flower R1,(a)
Drives my green age; that blasts the roots of trees R2,(b)
Is my destroyer. (a)
And I am dumb to tell the crooked rose R3 (b)
My youth is bent by the same wintry fever. (a)

The force that drives the water through the rocks R1 (c)
Drives my red blood; that dries the mouthing streams R2 (b)
Turns mine to wax. (c)

And I am dumb to mouth unto my veins R3 (b)
How at the mountain spring the same mouth sucks. (c)

The hand that whirls the water in the pool (R1)(d)
Stirs the quicksand; that ropes the blowing wind (R2)(b)
Hauls my shroud sail. (d)

And I am dumb to tell the hanging man R3 (b)
How of my clay is made the hangman's lime ..." (b)
(Dylan Thomas, from 'The force that through the green fuse...')

You can probably find some other patterns within the lines too.

Many modern poets, of course, mix the old and new systems together quite happily. What is being done here?

My father worked with a horse-plough,
His shoulders globed like a full sail strung
Between the shafts and the furrow.
The horses strained at his clicking tongue.

An expert. He would set the wing
And fit the bright steel-pointed sock.
The sod rolled over without breaking
At the headrig, with a single pluck

Of reins, the sweating team turned round
And back into the land. His eye
Narrowed and angled at the ground
Mapping the furrow exactly.
(Seamus Heaney, from 'Follower')

PRACTICAL WORK

1. Write a poem in rhymed couplets, titled 'Yes, But...' The lines are to start with these words alternately, and the rhythm should be regular. e.g.

   'Yes, your many words are kind and clear,
   But haven't told me what I want to hear.'

2. Invent or find a simple story with a strong plot which you can turn into a ballad. (Newspapers are a good source, with stories of heroic deeds, sporting exploits, tragic losses etc. You can alter names or any other details you wish.) Keep to reasonably regular metre and rhyme schemes, *abab* or two rhyming lines only. Try the effect of rhyming the first and third instead of the second and fourth. Does it work for you? If not, why?

3. Look at the poem you wrote after inventing a rhythm which you tested by clapping. Did you accent this rhythm with rhymes of one kind or another? Invent another rhythm, let the first words suggest themselves, then continue, using rhymes to mark the ends of lines. Don't worry about the sense of the poem - make it a nonsense one if you like. And use any kind of rhyme, full, near, or a mixture of both, whatever comes most naturally to you.

4. Produce a first draft of a poem by any means you like, using material from your notebook. Now re-write it twice, using full rhyme then half-rhyme. Which version comes closest to what you really mean to say? Could you combine the two to make an even better third version?

5. Think of something or someone that makes you angry. Write a stanza in iambic pentameter, rhyming *abab,* giving an example of this irritation. Add another stanza, rhyming *cdcd.* This could be a further example, or show how other people might be affected. Then think what good might come of this, or how the evil could be prevented, and put this down in six lines rhyming *efefgg.* With luck, you'll have written a sonnet. Does it come off? If not, could you make it fit the 'rules' better? Would writing more or less make it a better poem, though not a sonnet?

6. Now think of something or someone you love or admire. Write a poem without rhyme, but using repeated phrases in a regular pattern. The phrases can remain exactly the same, or change a little as the thought develops.

7. Find the exercise poem that you most enjoyed writing, or wrote with the least difficulty. Did it rhyme? Are there any other patterns that you can find in your writing that seem to come naturally to you? Write another with a different subject, but using the same system(s).

CHAPTER 5

IMAGINE THAT!

Some people might argue that the whole purpose of poetry is to give pleasure through imaginative experience, but let's step round a quicksand, and agree that imagery, which comes from and appeals to imagination, is simply a large component of any poem.

Yet what exactly is meant by *image* and poetic *imagery?* The words are more shifty than you might think, and I refer you to a dictionary for all definitions. But in common speech *image* means a representation of something: a photo of your cat, for instance. Once I have seen the photo, I have a good idea of what your cat is like, though she herself may be far away ambushing fieldmice. You could make the same image in words: – *black with white chest and paws, a kink in her tail.* Then I can 'see' her in my mind. You can add more, calling up my own cat-memories involving different senses: soft fur, sharp claws, loud mew. My own imagination might add extra things. She sometimes smells of fish, and feels heavy when she jumps on my lap.

Memories of all kinds of sensations are the raw material for creating images (visual, auditory, gustatory, olfactory, tactile, and kinaesthetic, if you like labels). Very often there are many elements in even a simple experience. For instance:

What did you have for breakfast? Was it tea and toast, porridge and salt, bacon and egg, croissant and jam, a bowl of cornflakes, just a cup of coffee? Whatever it was, you will probably be able to recall what it looked like, how it tasted, and perhaps little sounds associated with it. Maybe other memories too, based on other impressions. Healthy people use all their senses, but individuals vary in the ones habitually most favoured.

Many people think mainly in pictures. If you are one of these, breakfast is first a mental snapshot of, say, brown tea in a green cup, with two slices of toast, one slightly burnt at the edge, on a white plate. There's a slab of yellow butter in its dish beside the plate, and orange marmalade in a clear glass jar on the brown striped tablecloth.

Others often think in sounds. So, probably in association with a picture, there could be a memory of the splash of milk being poured, a scrunch of crisp cornflakes in the mouth, the metallic clink of the spoon in the sugar bowl.

Or perhaps taste, appropriately here, is very important to you? Then you may remember first the bland flavour of cooked oatmeal with the contrast of salt, or the buttery savour of croissant and sweetness of jam.

The sense of smell is closely connected with taste (which is why when you have a cold you can't taste properly). Your main recollection of breakfast might be the aroma of coffee beans and the tang of bacon wafting out of the frying pan.

Touch? You may recall the texture of the porridge on your tongue, the roughness of cornflakes, the warmth of coffee, as well as the cool smoothness of the plate and the bubbly waves of the seersucker tablecloth. Maybe the porridge was too hot, and you burnt your tongue, so you have a memory of pain, followed by the relief of a gulp of cold milk.

Some people will also remember the way their muscles worked in movement or effort, to lift a heavy teapot perhaps, or to reach across the table for the marmalade.

If you were writing a poem about breakfast, you would try to make the readers see, hear, smell, taste and touch so that the experience became vivid. In making an image, you hope that your words will re-create in your readers' minds almost the same impression that direct experience would have given, because you are re-awakening similar memories in them. Nevertheless you can also make them experience something new, by re-combining different components.

One could invent a different sort of ghost, for instance, out of simple elements – memories of a dead tree, a damp evening and an old man who had lost his money.

A phantom elm creaks through the wood
seeking old treasure, gold leaves,
weeping with mist.

Creating new images is perhaps the most fundamental of poetic skills. Understanding how it is done is a good first step, but it must be admitted that the sparks which jump between ideas, making an original synthesis, is intuitive. A gift. But even modest talent can develop remarkably with practice. In any case, if you're stuck it's worth trying the game of combining memories quite deliberately. A forced image may well lead you to a much better one.

Part of the secret is to be in the proper frame of mind. As you sit writing your draft give your right-brain self permission to reach in many directions, as in the popular technique of brainstorming, where all ideas – no matter how silly – are welcomed uncritically and not evaluated until later. Many of the images and ideas won't be any good, but that isn't important if you can find the one gem you need amongt the rubbish.

Because sight is so important to most people, visual images – verbal 'pictures' – are the most common, but your work will immediately become more interesting if you can also include images of sound, touch and so on. How many of your senses does this passage appeal to?

The barge she sat in, like a burnish'd throne,
Burn'd on the water; the poop was beaten gold,
Purple the sails, and so perfumed, that
The winds were love-sick with them, the oars were silver,
Which to the tune of flutes kept stroke, and made
The waters which they beat to follow faster,
As amorous of their strokes.
(Shakespeare, *Anthony and Cleopatra, II, 2*)

There are images of sight, of course. You must get a picture of a shining golden boat with purple sails and silver oars. Hearing too: the music of flutes, the sound of oars on water. Smell: the sails fill the very air with scent. There is a hint of touch in 'burnish'd' and 'burn'd', and more in the image of the amorous water eagerly pursuing the stroke of the oars. The beating oars also imply muscular effort driving the royal barge through the water.

There are no images of taste, though. These are comparatively rare in traditional poetry, but when they do occur they give a very sensuous effect. Here is a stanza from Keats' 'The Eve of St. Agnes'. Can you find images of sight, touch, and smell as well as the many of taste?

And still she slept an azure-lidded sleep,
In blanched linen, smooth, and lavender'd,
While he from forth the closet brought a heap
Of candied apple, quince, and plum, and gourd:
With jellies soother than the creamy curd,
And lucent syrops, tinct with cinnamon:
Manna and dates, in argosy transferr'd
From Fez; and spiced dainties, every one,
From silken Samarcand to cedar'd Lebanon.

To be successful, a poetic image must bear some kind of emotional charge for the reader. It must fit in with, and carry forward, the tone and theme of the poem as a whole. It must be clear, and sufficiently original to make your readers see, hear or taste with your eyes, ears and tongue. The image evoked by your words must persuade them to share your revelation, to experience things on your terms, and thus show them a new and vivid world.

Even if your poem-world is a sad one, the recognition of it, paradoxically, gives pleasure: the 'ah!' response, the feeling that 'I was there,' which you have built up by presenting a series of sense-impressions. This is similar to real life, which can only be experienced through the senses.

For this reason, avoid abstract expressions. If your words have nothing sensuous about them, think very carefully. The hard detail which brings something to life is far more telling than high-flying fog. If you want to express longing, for instance, give a concrete example: a child hoping for a bicycle, perhaps. Better still John wanting a 3-speed bike, painted red, complete with saddlebag, on Christmas morning.

Imagery occurs of course, in direct description:

Only a man harrowing clods
In a slow silent walk
With an old horse that stumbles and nods
Half asleep as they stalk.

(Thomas Hardy, from 'In Time of the Breaking of Nations')

Or here, but in this case with a hint that something more is meant than pure description of objects:

Monday I found a boot –
Rust and salt leather
I gave it back to the sea, to dance in.

Tuesday a spar of timber worth thirty bob.
Next winter
It will be a chair, a coffin, a bed.

(George Mackay Brown, from 'Beachcomber')

Figures of speech

Directness works well in narrative, giving an account of things apparently as they were. But sometimes this is not enough. You have to clarify meaning by making a comparison, that is by using figurative language, where literal meaning is put aside and true meaning is suggested obliquely.

Simile

When things are similar to each other, you can say they are like each other, or compare them with 'as'. In the Shakespeare passage above, the barge is likened to a throne. Here are some more examples:

She walks in beauty, like the night
Of cloudless climes and starry skies. (Byron)

*

And the sun comes up in the morning
Like barley-sugar on the water. (Louis MacNeice)

*

She is a procession no one can follow after
But be like a little dog following a brass band. (George Barker)

*

Pride like a goldfish flashed a sudden fin. (Edward Lucie-Smith)

*

[My love] is all as hungry as the sea
And can digest [as] much. (Shakespeare)

*

The cobwebs drooped heavy and hoar
As though with wool they had been knit. (Andrew Young)

The 'as' form is favoured in dozens of popular comparisons: *As bold as brass. As poor as a church mouse. As hot as hell. As cool as a cucumber. As white as (or whiter than) snow.* Because they are clichés, beware of using them. Find your own comparison instead.

Particularly in traditional poetry, extended similes give the poet a chance to produce striking images:

A savage place! as holy and enchanted
As e'er beneath a waning moon was haunted
By woman wailing for her demon-lover!
(Coleridge, from 'Kubla Khan')

Take care with this technique. This example fits in well with the mysterious, visionary atmosphere of the rest of the poem, itself forming a part of its texture. But used unskilfully the device can stick out incongruously, like angels' wings on a farmyard pig.

Another way is to use comparatives, saying that A is larger, smaller, something more or less than B. This may also give scope for imagery, like this:

There is sweet music here that softer falls
Than petals from blown roses on the grass,
Or night-dews on still waters between walls
Of shadowy granite, in a gleaming pass;
Music that gentlier on the spirit lies,
Than tired eyelids upon tired eyes.
(Tennyson, from 'Song of the Lotos Eaters')

Tennyson could have used similes: Music falls as softly as rose-petals, as softly as dew on mountain lakes; music that touches one as gently as closed eyelids. But it was more than this - softer and more gentle.

Metaphor

Metaphor also arises from a comparison of two things or qualities, but instead of saying A is like B, you say that A actually is B, as if one were superimposed upon the other.

All flesh is grass. (Bible, Isaiah.) [A is B]

The night sky is only a sort of carbon paper,
Blueblack, with the much-poked periods of stars
Letting in the light, peephole after peephole -
(Sylvia Plath, from 'Insomniac')

(Line One - A is B, Lines 2 and 3, B and A are described with further metaphors)

The two halves of a metaphor are called the *tenor,* which is the subject, and the *vehicle* which carries the comparison. So if flesh is grass, flesh (A) is the tenor and grass (B) the vehicle. The night sky is the tenor in the above, the carbon paper the vehicle, and the small holes made by full stops the vehicle for the tenor, the stars. Notice how the second metaphor follows neatly from the first.

Have a look at this, where metaphors of a shell-shaped ear and water are bound together:

The cathedral is God's
great whorled ear. Under
a roof of giant cockleshells
sung prayers stream
up, shoals of bright fish
flicking through water
over pebbles of stained glass.
(Michèle Roberts, from 'The Return')

In another type of metaphor, A behaves in the same way as B, or has B's attributes.

Old age, the squatter, found an unlocked life
and took possession

Here it's old age which takes possession, behaviour associated with a squatter. Metaphor of this sort is extremely common, in speech and written prose as well as poetry: *The wind roared through the trees.* (The wind behaves like a lion.) *A purring engine.* (The engine is a contented cat.) *Turn a blind eye.* (Ignore something, as Nelson treated the signal to disengage.) As you can see, the use of metaphor is not only more energetic, but more compact than a literal explanation. But take care not to let stale metaphors flatten your fizz.

Here are some more metaphors in action:

... the ivy's blunt webbed fingers (Andrew Young)

*

A spider's web, tense for the dew's touch,
A pail lifted, still and brimming – mirror
To tempt a first star to a tremor.
(Ted Hughes, from 'Full Moon and Little Frieda')

*

Lark drives invisible pitons in the air
And hauls itself up the face of space.
Mouse stops being comma and clockworks on the floor.
(Norman MacCaig from 'Movements')

Sometimes a metaphor emerges through parallels. The

reader must come to his own conclusion here:

She dwelt among th'untrodden ways
Beside the springs of Dove,
A maid whom there were none to praise,
And very few to love.

A violet by a mossy stone
Half-hidden from the eye!
Fair as a star, when only one
Is shining in the sky.
(Wordsworth, from one of the 'Lucy' poems)

From this, it is only a small step to an *extended metaphor* where the tenor may be present only in a vestigial form. Think about this short, complete poem:

His plumage is dun,
Talons long but blunt.
His appetite is indiscriminate.
He has no mate and sleeps alone
In a high nest built of brick and steel.
He sings at night
A long song, sad and silent.
He cannot fly.
(Vernon Scannell)

I have deliberately omitted the title for the moment. What is being described? At first you must think of a bird, given the clues of *plumage* and *talons*. A solitary bird, without a mate. The nest of brick and steel is a bit odd, isn't it? And a silent song is a contradiction, as are birds which cannot fly. The whole poem is a metaphor, creature B, standing for creature A. What could A be? Although it isn't intended as a riddle, it may be helpful to think of an extended metaphor in this way – and the answer is given on page 61 in the punning title.

The more elaborate your metaphors the more careful you must be to keep all parts congruent, or you end with an unsatisfactory *mixed metaphor* such as *The green shoots of recovery are looking bronzed and fit.*

Personification, Anthropomorphism
Another variation of metaphor is to speak to, or about, abstractions as if they were human.

> *O Wild West Wind, thou breath of Autumn's being* (Shelley)

> *Now at the last gasp of Love's latest breath,*
> *When, his pulse failing, Passion speechless lies,*
> *When Faith is kneeling by his bed of death,*
> *And Innocence is closing up his eyes ...*
> (Michael Drayton, from 'The Parting')

It is probably better nowadays to think of another way, rather than giving the abstraction a capital letter and hoping for the best. But if something animal, vegetable, mineral or abstract wants to behave in a human manner, treat it as just another metaphor: in 'Beachcomber' above, the sea was appropriately given the boot to dance in, though dancing is really something that only animate beings can do.

Metonymy and Synecdoche
Students of rhetoric have identified many figures of speech. If you are interested in language you may like to collect them, adding them to your notebook along with juice-filled words. But here I want to mention only two more.
Metonymy is the replacement of person or thing by a word associated with it: *the Bench* meaning the magistrates sitting on it, or *the Press,* signifying newspapermen or newspapers. *Synecdoche* is similar, naming a part instead of the whole. So you might speak of 'a hundred trunks' when you meant a hundred trees – or elephants. Both these figures are specialised forms of metaphor.

Symbols and Symbolism

Vernon Scannell's poem, which I used as an example of

extended metaphor, is called 'Jailbird'. If you now go back and read it again, you can see how describes a man locked away in prison in terms of bird behaviour and appearance. The prisoner is the tenor of the metaphor, the vehicle corresponding all the way through to aspects of his life. But suppose you didn't have a title to help you? The tenor of the metaphor would be missing. You would guess, I think, that more was meant by the poem than a description of a strange bird. You might suppose that it was a *symbol* carrying several possible connotations. For instance, it might stand for a mercenary soldier, dun in battledress, killing indiscrimately. It might stand for modern man in general, loveless and unable to be free. It might even stand for death, its song silent, unable to leave the ground. Or all of these.

Yet this is only my own reaction to the poem. Yours may well be different, and your interpretations quite as valid as mine. Poetic symbols are greatly expanded metaphors, and give an impression of depth, ambiguity and importance.

Here's the first stanza of Yeats' 'The Black Tower'. Do you feel an underlying meaning, beyond the face-value of the images? Or not?

Say that the men of the old black tower,
Though they but feed as the goatherd feeds,
Their money spent, their wine gone sour,
Lack nothing that a soldier needs,
That are all oath-bound men:
Those banners come not in.

It is probably better to let your symbols grow in your poetry in their own seasons, rather than trying to write in this way to start with. It also depends, very much, on how your own mind moves, if the materials of myth and archetype appeal strongly to you or not. Take care of images and metaphors, and the symbols will take care of themselves.

And there will be more about this in Chapter Eight.

PRACTICAL WRITING

1. Think of an ordinary experience, such as a journey to work or shopping trip. Jot down a few memories of different sense-impressions, including smells and tastes if you can. Transform these memories into images. Use them to write a straightforward descriptive poem, making it as vivid as you possibly can. (Don't forget the importance of rhythm, too.)

2. Write a rhymed poem with a proverb as its starting point. e.g. 'Look before you leap'. Translate the abstract advice into detailed imagery.

3. (a) Think of at least five objects and five people that you like or love. What quality about them makes you feel this way? Now think of other objects, people etc. that share the same qualities, and write down the resulting similes - e.g. 'My old brown coat's as comforting as cocoa.' 'Granny, like a firm, old house.'
(b) Do the same with things, people, feelings that you

dislike. e.g. 'A wind brutal as a breadknife.'
(c) For use later, put down a few things that are not like each other: remember Shakespeare's 'My mistress' eyes are nothing like the sun.'

4. Choose one of the banal similes in common speech, and change it into a metaphor. e.g. 'The paper as white as snow,' could become 'The snow of paper's whiteness.' Does the metaphor excite more imagery? e.g. 'Red ink splashed the snow of paper's whiteness...'

5. Now pick one of your own similes. Can you change it into a metaphor? Not all similes can be converted. 'The cocoa comfort of my coat...' No. I don't think that works well. When you find one that pleases you, use it as the basis of a short poem, letting appropriate metaphors follow on from this main one. Remember to use words in a suitable register too.

6. Choose some more of your similes but this time open them up into parallel phrases or sentences, e.g.

   'Granny, still tall, old-fashioned, strong.
   A stone house, indifferent to the wind.'

   If one of these pairs can be extended, or several of them fit well together, write the poem that they suggest.

7. (Difficult and optional) Write a sonnet, an extended metaphor, in which the tenor is given in the title, the vehicle forming the poem. A few ideas:

   Tenor: a lover. Vehicle: a plant of some kind.
   Tenor: an enemy or enemies. Vehicle: reptile(s) or insect(s).
   Tenor: river, mountain, mine or factory.
   Vehicle: a loved or hated human being.

   In the last suggestion, the inanimate feature will behave in a human way. Try to include images of different kinds, not only visual ones.

CHAPTER 6

WHAT KIND OF POETRY?

Of course you can't talk about 'poetry' as if it were the same kind of thing through and through. Poems, like animals, can be put into families, species, and classes. They may be useful or decorative, erotic or philosphical, earnest or funny. They are various.

If you have worked through the exercises at the end of each chapter, as recommended, you'll have drafted at least thirty poems, and perhaps begun to find your 'voice'. Looking over your work you'll probably find that some themes and strategies are repeated. But no poet is content to stick with the same kind of work for ever. Do you like writing about cities or nature? Fine, but don't stop there. Though you have to ask your poem *who are you and where are you going?* you ask it afresh with each beginning. What kind(s) of poet would you like to be? A brief run–through of a few different genres may help.

A related question is *Where could this poem be published (perhaps)?* In a magazine or paper? If so, which one? Radio? A reading in a pub or elsewhere? Set to music, classical or pop? Do you hope eventually to publish a collection or appear in an anthology? To have a chance of recognition, your poetry must fit an appropriate round or square hole.

Epic poetry

Some poetry of the past was shaped by social circumstances. The epic, for instance, celebrating the adventures of a great man, was sung or chanted to an audience likely to admire heroism. The hero's deeds (we might say today) contributed to the consciousness of that society, as each member shared in the myth. One of the earliest examples is the Babylonian

Epic of Gilgamesh. Gilgamesh was a partly divine king. His friend Enkidu was at first uncivilised, living like an animal, so that the epic seems to explore the total nature of man through the interaction of a god/man and man/animal. On Enkidu's death, Gilgamesh undertakes a quest to find immortality, hearing the story of the Flood on the way. As in many later tragedies, his inevitable failure is a noble one, leaving the audience exhilarated rather than depressed.

Other famous epics are the Greek *Iliad* which tells of the Trojan War, and *Odyssey* a story of the trials which beset Odysseus after the war was won. Virgil's Latin *Aeneid* continued to be admired through the Middle Ages, which produced its own epic: Dante's *Divine Comedy* where religious heroism replaced warlike exploits. Religion was also central to Milton's *Paradise Lost* and *Paradise Regained.* All these are full of the myths and stories which continue to underpin our own civilisation.

Are you an epic poet? Would it be possible to write such a poem today, even if you had the necessary years to spare? Would it become merely pastiche, or impossible to take seriously? Have the functions of epic poetry been taken over for ever by great novels, films and the theatre? It might be very interesting to find out...but leave it until you've become so well-known that anything you write is published automatically.

Poetic drama

The relationship between poetry and drama is a complex one. In Greece, poetry was the natural speech of theatre. Medieval miracle and morality plays were written in verse, and everybody has heard of Shakespeare. But there was a gradual drift to prose for play-writing, and it's only in this century that poetry has returned to the English stage, and colonised radio, as with Eliot, Louis MacNeice and Tony Harrison at this moment. Perhaps because television and film are specially suited to naturalism, the theatre no longer needs to be representational. Its glamour and illusion allow us to accept heightened language and symbolism. No need for elaborate sets or costumes, really. Words are the best colours, the best cloth.

Are you a poetic dramatist? You must try doubly hard, for you must learn theatrecraft as well as poetic skills. But all poets must have some sense of drama in any case, all dramatists a feeling for the rhythm and scope of language. Work at it, perhaps with one-act plays for local drama groups to start with.

Short poems versus long and narrative poetry

Nowadays poetry is shaped partly by the economics of publishing. Most poems are shortish, to fit into the corner of a paper, or not to outstay their welcome even in magazines devoted to poetry. These poems can be classified partly by their subject matter, partly by their tone - serious or light - partly by their form - ballad or sonnet, for instance. Longer narrative poems are still produced by established writers, such as Ted Hughes' *Gaudete,* and there are others, but younger poets with long stories to tell will most likely use prose.

Are you a narrative poet? Try your skill with ballads, and other shorter story poems before you embark on a long saga. Poetry for children might be something to consider.

Sequences

If you really want to write a long piece, perhaps about an idea seen from several points of view, a cycle or sequence is a practical compromise. The one subject can be explored through a series of linked poems. Each can be fairly short and offered separately if necessary.

Sonnets seem especially suited to cycles. Among celebrated examples are Sir Philip Sidney's 'Astrophel and Stella' and E.B. Browning's 'Sonnets from the Portuguese'. But you can experiment with other short forms. The important rule is to have unity of theme or subject.

Lyric poetry

A lyric is short and concentrates on one idea, usually the poet's own emotion. It was originally meant to be sung. Even today, when classifications are smudged, the lyric should sound musical. Almost all short love-poems fit this category, so there are plenty of examples, but it can exploit other states of mind too. One of my favourites is this one by Robert Graves, expressing the glory and terror of transience:

SICK LOVE

O Love, be fed with apples while you may,
And feel the sun and go in royal array,
A smiling innocent on the heavenly causeway.

Though in what listening horror for the cry
That soars in outer blackness dismally,
The dumb blind beast, the paranoiac fury.

Be warm, enjoy the season, lift your head,
Exquisite in the pulse of tainted blood,
That shivering glory not to be despised.

Take your delight in momentariness,
Walk between dark and dark, a shining space
With the grave's narrowness, though not its peace.

Songs

Plenty of lyrics are still intended to be sung, like pop-songs for instance. How about The Beatles' words? Do you perhaps remember Noel Coward, and Cole Porter? Are you a song-writer? Here is the place above all for skill in rhyme and regular rhythm, and for making colloquial language sound new.

Confessional poetry

Some unhappy poets use their work to express pain, often

acknowledging their own inner darkness. Several poets writing within the last twenty years felt so intolerably stressed that they ended in suicide. Even so, writing directly about such feelings may bring relief to the writer, and touch others too, because distress and disappointment are universal experiences.

Sleep at my side again, my bride,
As on our marriage bed you turned
Into a flowering bush that burned
All the proud flesh away. Beside
Me now, you, shade of my departed
Broken, abandoned bride, lie still,
And I shall hold you close until
Even our ghosts are broken hearted.
(From 'The True Confession of George Barker')

If you are a confessional poet, writing compulsively, advice may not be what you want. But if you can, put your work away for a while before its final revision, so that you can judge it more objectively than in the anger or misery of the moment. A touch of self-mockery or gleam of light may be needed as an artistic balance for gloom.

Daily I strolled through leaves to look for letters,
A half of bitter or a chance encounter.
My state was ecstasy, illusion, hunger,
And I was often lectured by my betters.

What wonder that I seldom rose till three
When light was leaking from the grimy primrose
That is the western sky of winter London,
Light in the head, lugubrious, cynical, free.
(Anthony Cronin, from 'Responsibilities')

Nature poetry

If you look at any anthology published up to about 1920, you will see that many of its poems are concerned with the natural world. The tradition started at a time when Middle English poets from chilly castles or colder hovels rejoiced in the coming of spring.

Sea, sky, river; mountain, moor and forest; lane and farmland, and all the creatures that walk, fly or swim give the nature poet an inexhaustible source of subjects. The snag is that so much has been written already that a poem which is purely descriptive may seem unoriginal, though acute observation may save it.

There are fewer poets of recent times who concentrate on nature – perhaps because so many people live urban lives. But there are still some, such as Andrew Young, R.S. Thomas, Ted Hughes and Geoffrey Grigson. But even these often give a symbolic twist to the season, scenery or animal, which is not simply described for its own sake. How, for instance, do you respond to the idea of reversal in this poem? Is it purely whimsical, or does it make you question the convention of up and down, under and over?

A DEAD MOLE

Strong-shouldered mole,
That so much lived below the ground,
Dug, fought and loved, hunted and fed,
For you to raise a mound
Was as for us to make a hole;
What wonder now that being dead
Your body lies here stout and square
Buried within the blue vault of the air?
(Andrew Young)

If you are primarily a nature poet should you try to suggest a further dimension through analogies or symbols? Or does nature seem complex enough already, not needing elaboration?

The contemporary concern with ecology is a 'new' subject, well worth trying, and (unlike the earth itself) not over-exploited yet.

Poems of place

Poems which have as their subject a particular location could be considered a sub-section of nature poetry, though towns are represented too.

You can't altogether pin these poems down, as many combine the idea of place with another theme, such as patriotism. This one, for instance, deals with nostalgia:-

Can I forget the sweet days that have been,
When poetry first began to warm my blood;
When from the hills of Gwent I saw the earth
Burned into two by Severn's silver flood:

When I would go alone at night to see
The moonlight, like a big white butterfly,
Dreaming on that old castle near Caerleon,
While at its side the Usk went softly by ...
(W.H. Davies, from 'Days that Have Been')

Perhaps you have a particular place you'd like to celebrate, or at least one which you know well? Poems can be about places that you dislike, too.

Poems about animals

Domestic animals also come under the 'Nature' heading. Almost all poets write about a cat or dog at some time, often at some length too. Where favourite animals are concerned, sentimentality is the main trap. Try to see the pet with a fresh eye. For instance, Stevie Smith accounts for a cat's bald patch by an encounter with an angel, which stroked it:

All the same I
Intend to go on being
A cat that likes to
Gallop about doing good
So
Now with my bald head I go,

Chopping the untidy flowers down, to and fro,
An' scooping up the grass to show
Underneath
The cinder path of wrath ...
(From 'The Galloping Cat')

Religious poetry

Anyone with a mystical nature will very likely be drawn towards poetry. (Though to love poetry is not necessarily to be a mystic.) Heightened and formal language has always been thought appropriate when speaking about great mysteries. If you belong to one of the organized religions, you must have absorbed much poetry already, as almost all the holy books of the world are written in poetic terms, and the symbols of a faith are already familiar to you.

Sincere devotion to God, like erotic love or overwhelming sadness, is one of the most compelling reasons for writing. The finished work is both an offering and an affirmation. There are abundant examples from all times and cultures, classical and modern.

From the Middle Ages onwards, there's a whole cathedral's worth of English Christian poetry, with Milton, John Donne, George Herbert, Hopkins, Fry and Eliot as perhaps the most obvious pillars; and more unorthodox pillars too, such as Blake, Coleridge, and Wordsworth.

Hymn-writing is a possibility, combining song with religion. A modern poet might well find a niche here, especially if you can write your own tunes or have a friend with whom you can collaborate.

The problem with writing any kind of religious poetry now is the same as with nature poetry. So much has been done already that deeply held faith is not enough. You have to think afresh, and at least consider expressing yourself in modern terms. 'Our Lady' by Mary Elizabeth Coleridge (1861- 1907) must have seemed startling in its time. This is how it begins:

Mother of God! no lady thou:
Common woman of common earth!
Our Lady ladies call thee now,
But Christ was never of gentle birth;
A common man of the common earth.

Would you retain the *thou* and *thee* today? Compare it with a couple of stanzas of Charles Causley's 'Ballad of the Bread Man':

Mary stood in the kitchen
Baking a loaf of bread.
An angel flew in through the window.
'We've a job for you,' he said.
...
It was election winter.
They went to vote in town.
When Mary found her time had come
The hotels let her down.

How do you react to the contemporary images and colloquial language? Does it belittle the subject for you or make it seem more real? Should there be a 'religious' register for religious poetry, even today? I don't ask because I think there is a yes or no answer. You must decide for yourself.

I use Christian verse only as an example. Other religions have great poetic traditions of their own. Or perhaps you have a New Age faith, feeling devotion to the Earth itself, which brings us back to nature poetry, and ecology; or maybe to older beliefs, shamanism, Wicca, Celtic fairy-faith or Magick, like Yeats:

Swear by what the sages spoke
Round the Mareotic Lake
That the Witch of Atlas knew,
Spoke and set the cocks a-crow.

Swear by those horsemen, by those women
Complexion and form prove superhuman ...
(from 'Under Ben Bulben')

Poetry itself has a close affinity with magic in its spell-binding, spell-making aspect, as Robin Skelton has pointed out. Controlled rhetoric is needed when speaking of, or to, powerful and mysterious forces. Poetry which has strong rhythm and rhyme has a quality of incantation. Similarly sacred chants and mantras are used to put one in tune with the divine.

Charms, spells, and incantations are all the province of the magician-poet. But take care. *They may work,* so be very sure you really want what you ask for, and heed the traditional warning not to wish others ill, in case the spell rebounds on its maker! A light touch is often acceptable too. Here's the first stanza of John Heath-Stubbs' 'A Charm against the Toothache':

Venerable Mother Toothache
Climb down from the white battlements,
Stop twisting in your yellow fingers
The fourfold rope of nerves;
And tomorrow I will give you a tot of whisky
To hold in your cupped hands,
A garland of anise-flowers,
And three cloves like nails.

Lyric poetry in all its variations is mainly personal, written from an individual's need to express - even exorcise - his feelings. Of course all poetry tends to reveal its author's emotions, but now let's look at a few categories that have a social function as well.

Occasional verse

Not what is produced by part-time poets! Just written for a special occasion, and intended for sharing with others for whom the time is significant. For instance, a Poet Laureate is, or was, meant to write verses to celebrate State events such as coronations and the ending of wars, but someone who can turn out a worthwhile poem in praise of the opening of a new Municipal Recycling Plant is following in the same tradition.

There are many occasions at work or in the family which might be improved by a spot of verse too: anniversaries, retirements, the birth of a child ... The greetings-card industry consumes large quantities of rhyming sentiment. Could you do better?

Practical verse

A rhyme is easier to recall than a piece of prose. So if people wanted to remember anything, especially in less literate times, they often used short verses of the 'Thirty days hath September' kind, as mnemonics. A few rhymes could be of real help to students for example, or anyone who needs to remember lists, dates, and facts.

Rhyme and regular rhythm are essential, so that the person repeating the verse can be certain nothing has been left out.

Elegies

The elegy has a very long history. Of course there are many lyric poems of mourning, such as:

> *I wish I were where Helen lies*
> *Night and day on me she cries,*
> *O that I were where Helen lies,*
> *On fair Kirconnell Lea!*
> (Anon. from 'Helen of Kirconnell')

but the difference between this and an elegy proper is formality. The elegiac poet may feel just as much sadness, but because the poem is intended as a public memorial, it usually moves to a slow and dignified rhythm. Milton's *Lycidas* was written after the drowning of Edward King, Tennyson's 'In Memoriam' after the death of Arthur Hallam. Both these poems have religious and philosophical overtones as well as lamenting the deaths of friends.

The term 'elegy' also covers a formal serious poem with a more general theme – Gray's 'Elegy Written in a Country Churchyard', for instance. Its dead were people whose potential both for good and evil had been unfulfilled.

Protest and complaint, anti-war poems.

Poems of protest have a public purpose too. They are often written from a political point of view, with the hope that an abuse of power or a social ill may be put right. For instance, Tom Earley's 'Instead of a Carol', which starts by rejecting the banal decorations of Christmas, continues:

Instead for us the exiled son of man,
New born in outhouse lying in the cold,
Though not for us one special holy boy
But everyone unwanted and unloved,
The lonely and the helpless and the poor
The little hungry child in every land.

Anti-war poems are similar in intention, emotion carried to an extreme in exposing horror. This century can provide all too many examples – the work of Wilfred Owen, Siegfried Sassoon, and Isaac Rosenberg among others in the First World War, Keith Douglas and Alun Lewis in the Second, and the CND generation of poets who worked to prevent the Third.

Their eyes sunk jellied in their holes
Were held up to the sun like begging bowls
Their hands like rakes with finger-nails of rust
Scratched for a little kindness from the dust.
To many, in its beak, no dove brought answer.
(Stephen Spender, from 'Memento')

If you are angry about injustice, poverty, violence and war, you may very well want to express your fury in poetry. It may help to feel you have done something to expose evil. But there is a pitfall here. 'The poetry is in the pity,' said Wilfred Owen, but it's easy to become too strident, to write propaganda rather than poetry. The test, I think, is to ask yourself 'Would this still be a fine poem if the cause were not a good one?' If yes, carry on, if no, perhaps you should use a different medium, not poetry, to express your opinions?

Satire

A satire is a poem of protest which uses ridicule, irony or sarcasm as well as anger to make its purpose clear. It's a great advantage if it's neat and memorable, but the motive of the poet is the reform of an abuse or exposure of a villain.

Probably nobody has wielded a lead sock more adroitly than Alexander Pope. Here is part of his celebrated attack on 'Sporus', identified as Lord Hervey:

> *Yet let me flap this bug with gilded wings,*
> *This painted child of dirt, that stinks and stings;*
> *Whose buzz the witty and the fair annoys,*
> *Yet wit ne'er tastes, and beauty ne'er enjoys...*
> (From 'Prologue to the Satires', lines 309-312)

Sometimes parody can be used effectively:

> *We spray the fields and scatter*
> *The poison on the ground*
> *So that no wicked wild flowers*
> *Upon our farm be found.*
> (John Betjeman, from 'Harvest Hymn')

If you have a gift for satire, there is plenty of material ready for your scalpel. One practical point, though - consider the laws of slander and libel before identifying individuals. People hate being found out, which is why satire still has real power.

Comic and light verse

This has to be witty and amusing, and is more good-natured

than satire. It pokes fun rather than stabs through the chest, though there may be an underlying serious message. Or it may be written simply from exuberance, a good-to-be-alive feeling. Its obvious purpose is to entertain, to cheer people up.

Edward Lear, Lewis Carroll, Byron, W.S. Gilbert, Hilaire Belloc, Ogden Nash, E.O. Parrott, Roger Woddis and Wendy Cope are merely a few of the thousands of such generous poets, and many at the very top have joined them occasionally, even such serious poets as Hardy, Yeats, Louis MacNiece, Auden and especially Betjeman. Perhaps times like ours demand poetry that scoffs at the pompous and rejoices in banana-skins.

The balance of amusing content and manipulation of language varies, of course, from poem to poem. Ideas first:

Professor Housman was I think the first
To say in print how very stimulating
The little ills by which mankind is cursed,
The colds, the aches, the pains are to creating;
Indeed one hardly goes too far in stating
That many a flawless lyric may be due
Not to a lover's broken heart, but 'flu.
(W.H. Auden, from 'Letter to Lord Byron')

Self-mockery is always a good bet:

I wish I owned a Dior dress
Made to my order out of satin.
I wish I weighed a little less
And could read Latin.
(Phillis McGinley, from 'Reflections at Dawn')

And then there is endless word-play, puns, games of all kinds:-

His death, which happen'd in his berth,
At forty-odd befell:
They went and told the sexton, and
The sexton toll'd the bell.
(Thomas Hood, from 'Faithless Sally Brown')

LIMERAIKU

There's a vile old man
Of Japan who roars at whores:
'Where's your bloody fan?'
(Ted Pauker)

If you have a bent for this kind of verse, you will probably find getting published is comparatively easy. But good light verse must be technically perfect. A faltering rhythm will spoil it, for instance. Keep a good book on prosody beside your bed.

A really funny poem may need twice as many drafts as a sad one - but will make you twice as many friends.

PRACTICE WRITING

1. Look back on the poems you have written so far. Do any subjects stand out as being particularly easy or painful to write about? Are there any that make you feel you are discovering something new about yourself or life in general?

   Have a quick look at the 'Checklist of Subjects' at the end of the book. Do any of these immediately strike you as being attractive, repellent, or challenging? Make lists under these three headings in your notebook. Choose one of each kind, and using a suitable form, write three short poems, making the imagery as vivid as you can. Do the difficult or painful one first, then reward yourself with the easy and exhilarating ones. You may feel release after having tackled a disturbing subject. Add to these lists as you find new things to write about.

2. Using free or blank verse, write a short dramatic dialogue using material from your ballad poem, or telling a new story. Keep to a fairly colloquial register.

3. Hum a favourite song, and once you have the air and rhythm firmly fixed in your mind, write new words for it. Parody old ones if you find it difficult to start with, then invent a completely new lyric. Let the music itself suggest a subject if possible.

4. Go out for a walk in the country or a park, noticing five interesting things about plants, animals or weather. Write down at least five images when you come home. Then work them into a poem, rhyming or not as you like, but so that anyone else would recognise the scene.

5. If you have a pet animal, invent three similes which will sum up its qualities, using the simile-making technique given in the last chapter. Convert them to metaphors or extended metaphors if you like, or leave them as they are, to form the basis for three stanzas.

   And/or imagine you own a mythological beast, such as a unicorn or basilisk, and continue as above.

6. Write a hymn and/or prayer to your God or Goddess,

using the language you think most appropriate to make it sound sincere but dignified. You could give thanks or ask for some material or spiritual blessing. Take care to keep the imagery vivid and avoid generalisation. If you don't believe in any religion at all, adopt a different persona and imagine that you do.

7. Is there anything that makes you furious on behalf of someone else? In prose, write a careful and accurate description of the evil, and especially its causes. Now, using a traditional form to give the impression of control, write a poem of protest or a satire to make the abuse clear to other people. Again, be careful to avoid generalisation.

8. Look in an anthology of light or comic verse until you find a poem that really makes you laugh. Try to account for this. Is there a funny situation? Is there a built-in anti-climax? Does the poem depend on puns, double-entendres or other linguistic cleverness? Write a poem of your own with similar device(s) but a different plot.

CHAPTER 7

EXACTLY WHAT I SAID

Congratulations. By now you should be comfortable with the basic tools of the poet's kit. You know the best conditions for your mind to produce ideas, and you respect the subtleties of language. You are sensitive to rhythm and rhyme and starting to produce imagery for particular results. You know which kinds of poetry you find easy or difficult. You are keeping a notebook of useful raw material.

From now on, it's Everest all the way. An exhilarating thought.

As with any other craft, once you have made a good start you begin to realise how very much more there is to it. If you achieve one effect, it is at the expense of something else, and the poem you intend to write is always better than the one you actually produce. No matter how high you climb, the path still goes on up. Even if you're a reincarnation of Shakespeare, there is always scope for refinement of technique to get closer to what you meant to say. Accordingly this chapter will cover some of the challenges of revision.

Titles

A title gives an important first impression, ideally intriguing the reader and summarising the subject or theme. The Trade Descriptions Act doesn't yet apply to poetry, but a fair and helpful title is something to aim for. A difficult poem can be made easier to understand if you give a clue to start with. On the other hand, even a good poem can stay unread if the title is boring. As a general rule avoid foreign words, which can sound pretentious, and any which are obscure or difficult to pronounce. Readers don't like being made to feel ignorant.

Power of the concrete –

I have already urged you to keep images clear and detailed, and to remember that imagery can involve all the senses, not merely sight. But in early drafts, when you are in a hurry to get down general ideas, it is common to find vague nouns rather than the specific ones which would give harder focus. Consider this:

PRELUDE (WICKLOW)

Still south I went and west and south again,
Through Wicklow from the morning till the night,
And far from cities and the sites of men,
Lived with the sunshine and the moon's delight.

I knew the stars, the flowers, and the birds,
The grey and wintry sides of many glens,
And did but half remember human words,
In converse with the mountains, moors, and fens.
(J.M. Synge)

Pleasing word-music, I grant. But now compare it with this:-

Old Meg she was a gipsy;
And lived upon the moors,
Her bed it was the brown heath turf,
And her house was out of doors.
Her apples were swart blackberries,
Her currants, pods o' broom;
Her wine was dew of the wild white rose,
Her book a churchyard tomb.
Her brothers were the craggy hills,
Her sisters larchen trees;
Alone with her great family
She lived as she did please.
(Keats, from 'Meg Merrilies')

Which poem are you likely to remember better next year?

– But don't overdo it

However, where poetry is concerned, any rules are likely to be provisional. You *can* have too much detail. For example, Wordsworth probably meant to sound accurate when describing the pool where a baby was drowned:

I've measured it from side to side
'Tis three feet long and two feet wide.
(From an early version of 'The Thorn')

He had second thoughts. William McGonagall didn't, but left his celebration of 'The Newport Railway' as it was:

...[It] will clear all expenses in a very short time
Because the thrifty housewives of Newport
To Dundee will often resort,
Which will bring them profit and sport,
By bringing cheap tea, bread and jam,
And also some of Lipton's ham ...

McGonagall was aiming at a serious poem. His list is specific. His thinking is politically correct - from both capitalist and social points of view. But does it come off? If not, why?

Do any of your images have associations which clash with the general feeling of the poem? All images, the tone, and the register of the words must work together. Even a particularly splendid image may need to be cut if it doesn't fit in. (Don't waste it though. Use it elsewhere.)

If the inappropriate image is also trivial, you must be really tough and prune it away completely. Anti-climax is a good device for comic effect, but when it is unintentional it's known as *bathos*. Even a small pinch of it will ruin a poem, like putting salt instead of sugar in your tea.

Imagist and 'Martian' techniques

If you have trouble in creating clear images, I suggest you pay special attention to two groups of poets, the Imagists who flourished in the early part of this century, and the Martian school of a few years ago, named after Craig Raine's collection *A Martian Sends a Postcard Home.*

The Imagists included T.E. Hulme, Hilda Doolittle (H.D.),

Ezra Pound and D.H. Lawrence. Pound and Lawrence especially developed further, but the methods of the imagists are still worth trying. They insisted on direct treatment of the subject and on cutting out any words that were not essential. (They also wrote in musical phrases, rather than mechanically in poetic feet, as described already in Chapter 3, 'free verse'.) Their poems tended to be short, lyrical, and sometimes influenced by classical Greek models. They admired and emulated Japanese forms too, such as haiku and tanka, and invented similar short forms of their own.

ALBA

As cool as the pale wet leaves
of lily-of-the-valley
She lay beside me in the dawn.
(Ezra Pound)

Their observation was close and description accurate:

BEGGAR

In the gutter
piping his sadness
an old man stands,
bent and shrivelled,
beard draggled,
eyes dead.

Huddled and mean,
shivering in threadbare clothes -
winds beat him,
hunger bites him,
forlorn, a whistle in his hands,
piping.

Hark! the strange quality
of his sorrowful music,
wind from an empty belly

wrought magically
into the wind –

pattern of silver on bronze.
(F.S. Flint)

The 'Martian' has a way of looking at things as if for the first time, as a space-traveller might when exploring a new planet. If you can imagine you are a week-old baby with an adult vocabulary, you might get the same effect.

In homes, a haunted apparatus sleeps,
that snores when you pick it up.

If the ghost cries, they carry it
to their lips and soothe it to sleep

With sounds. And yet, they wake it up
Deliberately, by tickling with a finger.
(Craig Raine, from 'A Martian Sends a Postcard Home')

So you might see, but not comprehend, a thing which the natives call a telephone. This is an extreme example of the method, but looking with an innocent eye leads to some strikingly original and exact images:

Seven striped shallots are giving
a silent recital on their sitars
(from 'Shallots')

The boy turns to offer me
a miniature organ of cigarettes ...
(from 'The Trout Farm')

In the dormitory, boys laced up
their rugby boots like parcels,

knowing the mud outside would add
that final touch of sealing wax.
(from 'Memories of the Linen Room')

Using negatives creatively

In poetry, negative statements are often important and interesting. You must consider exactly how they will affect the reader, because it is impossible for the human mind not to visualise something once it has been mentioned.

For example, suppose I describe a poor child's birthday: she had no presents tied with ribbon, a single currant bun instead of a pink iced cake, and no balloons – not one, neither red nor green. You are certain, I think, to have seen in your mind's eye a beribboned gift, both bun and pink cake, and red and green balloons. Logically, all except the bun are absent, but they are present in your imagination, and the effect lies in making you see the contrast between what could have been and what was actually there.

A plain without a feature, bare and brown,
No blade of grass, no sign of neighbourhood,
Nothing to eat and nowhere to sit down,
(W.H. Auden, from 'The Shield of Achilles')

You can affirm something by drawing attention to it with a negative:

Nothing I cared, in the lamb white days, that time would take me
Up to the swallow thronged loft by the shadow of my hand,
In the moon that is always rising,
Nor that riding to sleep
I should hear him fly with the high fields
And wake to the farm forever fled from the childless land.
(Dylan Thomas, from 'Fern Hill')

A very valuable device, this. Dylan Thomas was able to change direction without openly contradicting the poem's prevailing mood of childhood happiness.

Conditional phrases are often used in the same way. Here a conditional follows the negatives for even more obsessive contrast:

Here is no water but only rock
Rock and no water and the sandy road
The road winding above among the mountains
Which are mountains of rock without water
If there were water we should stop and drink
Amongst the rock one cannot stop or think ...
(T.S. Eliot, from *The Waste Land* V.)

A negative or conditional can be useful in shaping a paradox too:

I could not love thee, dear, so much,
Loved I not honour more.
(Richard Lovelace, from 'To Lucasta, Going to the Wars')

In the exercise in simile-making at the end of Chapter Five, I suggested you should think of a few things which were unlike each other - an 'unsimile', to invent a name for it. This is a cheerful device, which can be exploited in several ways. 'My mistress' eyes are nothing like the sun,' said Shakespeare, arousing one's curiosity - well, what are they like, then? He was mocking a fashion for exaggeration.

You can also easily get into surrealism:

Not like a Black Hole juggling oranges
Not like the desert that breaks down the door...

Thus when you start to revise a poem, look very closely at all the negative statements, to make sure that the effect you are getting is the appropriate one. Negatives can actually add to richness of texture.

Don't preach

Didactic poetry, that is the kind with a moral message, is out of fashion. You may sincerely believe you have the answer to all mankind's ills, especially if you are writing religious or protest poetry, but even if you are right you may irritate your readers profoundly if you tell them directly a) what to think, or b) how to behave:

Be good, sweet maid, and let who can be clever;
Do lovely things, not dream them, all day long.
(Charles Kingsley, from 'A Farewell')

If you have a strong urge to alter the world, present your reasoning as a personal story. For example, as Herbert does in 'The Collar'.

If you have a point you want to get across, and can't do it by presenting the evidence and leaving it at that, you could try asking leading questions:

When the stars threw down their spears,
And water'd heaven with their tears,
Did He smile His work to see?
Did He who made the lamb make thee?
(William Blake, from 'The Tiger')

A similar temptation is to round off a poem with a moral, or at least to underline what you have already said. Even very good poets give way sometimes:

He prayeth best, who loveth best
All things both great and small;
For the dear God who loveth us,
He made and loveth all.
(Coleridge, from 'The Rime of the Ancient Mariner')

If you find yourself doing this, work backwards from the end, cutting out anything that repeats what you have already implied. Very often you'll find a good ending at a strong image, just before you began summing up.

Language!

Should you use 'taboo' words in your poems, or not? These are simply words which society has agreed are immoral or blasphemous. They used to be considered literally unprintable. But there is nothing at all startling in the sounds themselves. Similar words are in common usage: grit, hunt, rock, luck...

As with all words, you must judge if they are appropriate, and convey the right tone for your particular poem. Do you want to shock? Do they fit the persona? If so, use the most colourful expressions you know, but not just to sound trendy. They are valuable in their own way. Don't weaken them by over-use.

Style

There *are* some words and phrases though, which should be off-limits.

Clichés as described on page 19, have strong roots and need pulling up whenever you come across them.

Archaic words sometimes creep in without your noticing, under the influence of traditional Eng. Lit. They were perfectly acceptable in the past, but you should only use them now if you are deliberately writing pastiche or need an old-fashioned tone for a special purpose. Otherwise cut out *thee, thou, 'twas, e'er, ne'er, nay, yea* and any similiar words that you wouldn't use in writing an ordinary letter, or in speech. Be suspicious of direct address to any abstraction, especially if you start *O* as in 'O Grief' or 'O Joy'. In fact be suspicious of 'O' anything.

There are also vague *qualifiers* which wrap cotton-wool round your thoughts, often because you are trying to be honest. '*Quite* a tall tree'. '*Fairly* exciting'. '*Rather* horrible'. Even *very* and *extremely* are probably better left out. How does this strike you?

Blow, blow a bit, thou somewhat wintry wind,
Thou art not quite so unkind,
As man's extreme ingratitude;
Thy tooth is not really so keen,
Because on the whole thou art not seen
Although I must admit thy breath be rude.
(Katherine Knight. Apologies to Shakespeare)

Adjectives and adverbs can be like vampires sucking the life-blood from your verse. Almost all poets start by using too many - look at the early work of Keats or Hopkins for instance. Again, it is because you are trying to tell the whole truth. But the pace of a poem is more important. The sense and flow are carried forward by nouns and verbs. The adjectives you need are those required for the image, not to pad the line. Notice for instance how few adjectives there are at the beginning of Robert Frost's 'After Apple-picking':

My long two-pointed ladder's sticking through a tree
Toward heaven still,
And there's a barrel that I didn't fill

Beside it, and there may be two or three
Apples I didn't pick upon some bough.
But I am done with apple-picking now.
Essence of winter sleep is on the night,
The scent of apples: I am drowsing off.

The ladder is made particular, and it is *winter* sleep that follows the harvest, but apart from that the story unfolds quickly and naturally.

So look hard at every single adjective and adverb you have used. If they add little, or slow down the momentum, do away with them, even if it means rewriting for the sake of rhythm or rhyme. Let me stress though, that some poetry *does* require a fair number of adjectives, as Hopkins' did. Just be sure.

Look at the length of your sentences. It's worth wondering if you could cut a long one into two or three. If you have a lot of sub-clauses your reader may get bogged down. The more main verbs you have the quicker the movement, and the easier it is to follow. Are the sentences written in a natural word-order? Sometimes you may want to alter the expected structure for the sake of emphasis, but please avoid *inversion* of noun and adjective, especially if it's to make a rhyme.

And excuse me, but is your writing grammatical? If not, is this careless or intentional? By all means push syntax and punctuation to see what will happen, like e.e. cummings:

Lifting the valleys of the sea
my father moved through griefs of joy;
praising a forehead called the moon
singing desire into begin
(from 'my father moved through dooms of love')

– Or like Don Marquis's *archy and mehitabel,* a cockroach and alley-cat inhabited by the souls of a *vers libre* poet and Cleopatra respectively: Archy couldn't work the shift-key on the typewriter. But for maximum effect, you must know the conventions before you destroy them. Get a good guide to modern English usage anyway.

Checking through poetry is always worth doing, though it's often painful to alter what you wrote with passion. When you have done your best, a writing circle or friendly fellow-poet can help enormously by giving you an honest second opinion. But learn when to stop. Over-revision can destroy freshness. Keep your drafts, too, in case you want to go back to an earlier version. Beware of the habit of over-writing on a word processor, without saving first.

It's better not to mix creation and revision in the same session. Keep the unquestioning creative mood for writing, a more objective mood for constructive criticism. Both are necessary. As an editor you are your own best friend, helping to get as close as possible to the perfect poem you intended.

PRACTICAL WORK

1. Find your least successful poem. Imagine it was written by someone who has asked your opinion about it. Read it both silently and aloud, going through a checklist: title, subject, tone, imagery, appropriate language, style, form, rhythm, rhyme (if used) and word-music in general. Which aspect(s) could be better? Once you have made a careful diagnosis, rewrite the poem as many times as necessary until you are proud of it, perhaps putting it away for a few days between each draft.

   In future, look through all your work after an interval, to see if it could possibly be improved.

2. Find a poem or single stanza in an anthology which you feel is too generalised to be interesting. Rewrite it, keeping the basic idea but using plenty of sensuous imagery to make it memorable.

3. Write an imagist and/or Martian poem. Suggested subjects: a town sparrow, a bus, a walk in the rain, peeling potatoes, a children's game such as marbles, visiting a hospital.

4. Think of a character or situation involving deprivation, such as a homeless person, a loveless relationship or an ugly place. Write a poem using a lot of negatives, contrasting the plenty which might have been with the actual lack.

5. Consider the 'unsimiles' you wrote as part of Exercise 3, Chapter Five. Continue the train of thought to make a surreal (or nonsense) poem. E.g. *My kitten isn't like a bee, it's more like cactus or a flea.* Think of some 'unmetaphors' too, and do the same with them. E.g. *A butterfly is not a wish, though both have wings...*

6. (Easier) Using one of your own free–verse poems, go through it and cut out all adjectives. If necessary for the sense, substitute similes or metaphors instead. E.g. instead of 'grey, towering clouds' try 'clouds like cliffs'. Rewrite to preserve the rhythm you had, adding new material or shortening as appropriate.
   (More difficult) Write a lyrical poem in a traditional form with no adjectives and only three adverbs.

CHAPTER 8

EXTRA DIMENSIONS

Poetry has grown more complex over the last hundred years. Since Freud and Jung, art of all kinds has become a concern of psychology, and in return psychology has been raided to provide raw material for art. The work of the Symbolists and Surrealists particularly has had a profound influence, pictorial art and poetry sharing inspiration from dreams and archetypal symbols.

Before this, poetic imagery was usually held firmly in a frame of rational meaning. There was a story, or at least an easily understood situation, or a moral or metaphysical discussion. Literal and imaginative interpretations worked together. But as poetry comes closer to psychoanalysis, the neat frame crumbles and the imagery falls into different patterns, like a kaleidoscope. Thus some poetry has become shifting, multi-layered, ambiguous and difficult. To 'understand' it one must enter the same kind of consciousness as the writer's, allowing the imagery which has emerged from a deep part of the poet's mind to sink equally deeply into one's own. Exactly how true this is depends on individuals, of course, and there seems to be a revolt against very obscure poetry at the moment.

As far as a new poet is concerned it means that a modern sophisticated audience often expects highly concentrated work, which may be written on several levels or with multiple meanings – the 'extra dimensions' of my chapter heading. In a way we have returned to the cleverness of the Middle Ages and Renaissance, but with a different emphasis.

If you think this 'difficult' poetry is not, or not yet, the kind you want to write, fine. It is advanced in every sense of the word, and many good poets prefer a simpler mode and a wider audience. All the same, it may be interesting to think of a few ways to make your poetry more condensed, and some of the 'layering' devices which underlie modern and past practice.

Advanced imagery

Images can be made more startling and original by several methods. One interesting way is to use *synaesthesia* where a sense-impression is given in terms of a different one – vision/sound, for instance:

An' the dawn comes up like thunder outer China 'crost the Bay!
(Kipling, from 'Mandalay')

Or touch/vision:

Already he can feel daylight, his white disease.
(Sylvia Plath, from 'Insomniac')

Or smell/hearing:

The smell of mince pies, like a Christmas song

These are original, but the principle is found in ordinary speech, as when we say 'a rasping voice' (touch/hearing) or 'a warm colour' (touch/sight) and so on.

Looking through telescope or microscope may give you new ideas too – I call it the 'Gulliver effect', or seeing the world in a grain of sand. If you make something either much bigger or smaller, new images may strike you. Sylvia Plath again, for instance, thinking of blood corpuscles after she cut her thumb:

Out of a gap
A million soldiers run,
Redcoats, every one.
(From 'Cut')

Another device to hold your readers' attention is *paradox,* a statement which taken at face-value seems to contradict itself or be impossible: 'The Child is father of the Man' for instance, as Wordsworth said. Wrong way round, you think at first, until you work out that he meant the child comes before the man, or the man's character follows from the child's. It may be a good idea to set up a paradox before you present it:

Or, your owne end to Justifie,
For having purpos'd change, and falsehood; you
Can have no way but falsehood to be true?
(Donne, from 'Woman's Constancy')

A good modern example is the start of Andrew Motion's 'The Legacy':

Ashes have scattered her,
Her money disowns her.

This is ingenious writing, but moving too. Because her ashes were scattered, so was she. Because her money is now owned by her heirs, it has no more to do with her. The sense of loss is clear.

Oxymoron is similar, two apparently incompatible things being linked together. Milton's powerful phrase 'darkness visible', depicting the unholy illumination of Hell, is an example.

Metaphor further extended

The principle of extended metaphor has already been described in Chapter Five, but because it shades into symbolism, so important in modern poetry, it deserves further consideration.

Another way of understanding how to use this kind of metaphor is to make a distinction between the subject and the theme of a poem. The subject is what it is about (the vehicle) the theme is the underlying message (the tenor).

As an example of a poem on at least two levels lets look at 'Worm Within' by Anthony Thwaite. What does the title mean, to start with? What worm, and what is it within? The poem starts by giving an answer on the literal level. There is a wooden doll which contains a wood-boring insect. The sound it makes is at first, significantly, thought to be within the poet:

WORM WITHIN

A souvenir from Sicily on the shelf:
A wooden doll carved out of some dark wood,
And crudely carved, for tourists. There it stood
Among the other stuff. Until one night,
Quietly reading to myself, I heard
It speak, or creak - a thin, persistent scratch,
Like the first scrape of a reluctant match,
Or unarticulated word
That made me look for it within myself

As if I talked to myself. But there it was,
Scratching and ticking, an erratic clock
Without a face, something as lifeless as rock
Until its own announcement that it shared
Our life with us. A woodworm, deep inside,
Drilled with its soft mouth through the pitch-stained wood

[The presence of the destroyer takes on deeper significance:]

And like the owl presaging death of good,
Its beak closing as the dynasty died,
It held fear in those infinitesimal jaws.

[Then the poem returns to the literal everyday level for a few lines before urgency is felt with a suggestion that the insect might be as dangerous as the Trojan Horse was to Troy:]

So - to be practical - we must choose two ways;
Either to have some expert treat the thing
(Trivial, absurd, embarrassing)
Or throw it out, before the infection eats
The doors and floors away: this Trojan horse
In miniature could bring the whole house down,

I think to myself wildly, or a whole town...

[Finally comes a rhetorical question that expands the anecdote into something of even more importance, hinting at much greater corruption:]

Why do we do nothing, then, but let its course
Run ticking, ticking, through our nights and days?

The title now can be read in two senses, literally woodworm in a doll, metaphorically a rottenness which 'we' – mankind in general? – do nothing to counteract. If you supply your own ideas of the nature of the decay, the worm starts to become a symbol instead of a metaphor, with multiple connotations.

Putting it another way, the subject is woodworm in a doll, the theme, man's inability to cope with his flawed nature (or something along those lines).

Conceits

Nothing to do with vanity in this context, a *conceit* is an extended metaphor which is specially whimsical, fantastic or playful. Examples abound in Elizabethan and metaphysical poetry. Here for instance John Donne is elaborating on the significance of a flea sharing both his and his lady's blood:

Oh stay, three lives in one flea spare,
Where wee almost, yea more than maryed are.
This flea is you and I, and this
Our mariage bed, and mariage temple is;
Though parents grudge, and you, w'are met,
And cloystered in these living walls of Jet.
(from 'The Flea')

Conceits are suitable for an intellectual kind of poetry, because the more far-fetched they are the less emotion they convey. Readers are likely to think 'How ingenious!' rather than 'How moving!'

Allegory

Allegory was loved especially by educated medieval people. They got two poems for the price of one, because in this form an obvious story runs parallel to a metaphorical one. 'The Romaunt of the Rose', translated from French, or Langland's 'The Vision Concerning Piers Plowman' are examples. Spenser's 'Faerie Queene', which referred to Elizabeth I, pushed the form to its limit, even though only half of the projected work was completed. It was to have followed the adventures of heroes personifying twelve 'Morall vertues'. Thus the first book, 'The Legende of the Knight of the Red Crosse', represents Holiness in action like an Arthurian knight, overcoming evil to rescue and marry Una, or Virtue, in a happy ending. It can be read simply as a melodious narrative, but it also sustains a moral meant to be taken seriously.

Shorter allegorical pieces can be still be written successfully, though you may think of them, too, as extended metaphors. In Sylvia Plath's 'Mirror' for instance, the literal level describes the function of a looking-glass (which turns into a lake in the second stanza). But the allegory is of time and the impersonal destruction it causes:

I am silver and exact. I have no preconceptions.
Whatever I see I swallow immediately
Just as it is, unmisted by love or dislike.
I am not cruel, only truthful –
...
Now I am a lake. A woman bends over me,
Searching my reaches for what she really is.
...
I am important to her. She comes and goes.
Each morning it is her face that replaces the darkness.
In me she has drowned a young girl, and in me an old
woman
Rises toward her day after day, like a terrible fish.

Symbolism

There is a natural progression, as I have hinted before, from simile -> metaphor -> extended metaphor -> symbol, all devices by which one thing can be defined, described or evoked by something else. A symbol in poetry is like a metaphor, but wheras the metaphor has a tenor and vehicle, the symbol is all vehicle. It is like a metaphor with the carpet pulled from under its feet, leaving the reader to intuit what the tenor might be. Frequently there are many interpretations, all valid, giving the poem an impression of mystery and richness hinting at great underlying truths waiting to be discovered.

But ambiguity has disadvantages too. If there is no strong guiding thread through the labyrinth, the Minotaur may get you. 'Meaning' in the ordinary sense can be so obscured that ordinary sensible people decide poetry is incomprehensible and they'd rather watch TV. A poem is not a crossword puzzle with cryptic clues to meaning, and the poet who naturally uses symbolism has a duty, I think, to be as clear as possible. However, if the thought is complex, and can only be expressed through personal symbols, then the reader is justifiably asked to use sympathy and intelligence to grasp the poem's significance.

Symbolism runs through a spectrum, in common use at one end, and idiosyncratic at the other. Most symbolism in poetry is somewhere between the two. 'Public' symbols are commonly understood by most people sharing a particular culture. These are the ones you will find in a dictionary of symbols, and include archetypes, basic units of the human psyche everywhere, according to Jung. Thus it is easy to see that light/darkness, or day/night, are symbolic of such abstractions as good/evil, understanding/ignorance, life/death, reason/intuition and so on.

Some are more slanted to particular groups. For instance, the serpent in Christian myth can signify the Devil, himself a personification of evil. In other systems however, the serpent has connotations of death and/or rebirth and renewal, fertility, especially through its phallic aspect, and mediation between earth and underworld. In D.H. Lawrence's 'Snake' these ideas move beneath the surface of apparent description, as in these few lines:

And truly I was afraid, I was most afraid,
But even so, honoured still more
That he should seek my hospitality
From out of the dark door of the secret earth.
...
A sort of horror, a sort of protest against his
withdrawing into that horrid black hole,
Deliberately going into the blackness, and slowly
drawing himself after,
Overcame me now his back was turned.

He threw a log at the water-trough where the snake had been, but immediately regretted his action.

And so, I missed my chance with one of the lords
Of life.

Sometimes symbolism of the public kind is reinterpreted by the poet, given a personal colour, hinting at much but still easy to respond to. For example in 'The North Ship' Philip Larkin uses the symbol of ships to express - what? Clearly some kind of journey: through life itself? through difficulty? into a spiritual dimension? Let the poem explain itself.

I saw three ships go sailing by, *[notice the*
Over the sea, the lifting sea, *quotation from*
And the wind rose in the morning sky, *a carol]*
And one was rigged for a long journey.

The first goes westwards 'to a rich country', the second east, 'to anchor in captivity', while the third travels north.

East and west the ships came back
Happily or unhappily:

But the third went wide and far
Into an unforgiving sea
Under a fire-spilling star,
And it was rigged for a long journey.

But some poets go all the way, their symbolism so personal that it can be difficult to approach in any way. Here above all as a reader you have to let the poetry wash over you, experiencing it rather than trying to grasp it rationally. Much of Yeats, some of Eliot, Pound, Dylan Thomas, Sylvia Plath and many others in the mid-century is of this kind. They are pioneers, renewing poetry from within. In a hundred years what they 'meant' will seem obvious, because their work is already settling into educated consciousness, as Hopkins' has done, though it too was considered very difficult when first published.

Yet as a writer of this kind of poetry, you must be prepared to put up with a great deal of incomprehension, discouragement, and even ridicule. This is because it is in this area that much bad poetry is written, unnecessarily ambiguous, self-indulgently obscure and pretentious. As with confessional poetry, put it away and see if you still like it later on.

Eliot's 'Objective correlative'

Here in Eliot's own words is his theory:

> The only way of expressing emotion in the form of art is by finding an 'objective correlative'; in other words, a set of objects, a situation, a chain of events which shall be the formula of that *particular* emotion; such that when the external facts, which must terminate in sensory experience, are given, the emotion is immediately evoked.
>
> (from 'Hamlet' in *Selected Essays*)

Many critics have argued about it, but to my mind this is a kind of symbolism. Let's work backwards for a moment: the end is the sensory experience which results in the emotion. You have seen already how an image which refers to the senses makes you feel present in the experience. For example, if I mention strong wind and rain stinging your face while you are at sea by yourself in a small boat, the sail split, you might imagine yourself cold and wet, lonely and afraid. So if I wanted to express the emotions of loneliness and fear, the storm at sea might be a formula to evoke them, or the 'objective correlative'. No mention need be made of fear or loneliness in the poem, which concentrates on the force eight gale and the cracking mast.

But I think it a mistake to think of it as a formula. Most people might be frightened in the storm, but not someone used to rounding Cape Horn single-handed! As always in poetry, the reader brings his own luggage.

Does it hold true of Eliot himself? Do you think Eliot's own work is easier to understand if you read it with the principle of the objective correlative in mind? I leave you to decide.

Drawing on literary context

Whatever you write today will be judged against the whole backdrop of Eng. Lit., and even the humblest poem in a parish magazine will be slotted into a hierarchy, subconsciously, by its readers. In other words, you cannot write in a vacuum. Many poets use this situation to their advantage, by alluding to or using pre-existing work as another way of adding an extra dimension to their own.

At its simplest, you can use or adapt well-known phrases, proverbs and even well-chosen clichés.

'Once below a time' said Dylan Thomas, altering only one word in the traditional opening of a fairy story. Because the *below* is unexpected, it stands out in contrast to *upon*. So this example conveys, I think, a feeling of a sinister, underworld fairy-story about to begin.

Sometimes you can adapt even nursery rhymes. For example 'Roses are red, violets are blue' is far from childish here:

> *But her roses were never red,*
> *white rather, the colour of cold sheets, of piled snow,*

of paper unwritten on. A spread
of silence. 'And my violets are for sale, you know,'
the little match girl cried.
(Jane Kingshill, from 'A Valentine for Ophelia')

Allusion and quotations

If you use phrases that belong to our common cultural stock – such as lines from Shakespeare, the Bible, or a famous poet, they resonate with the original context and will have strong associations for many of your readers.

Quotation is one of the fine tools at your disposal, but be careful when you use it. Firstly, there are laws against plagiarism (see below). Secondly, you must be quite sure that the allusion reinforces and doesn't cancel what you are trying to say. It's no good to quote a line because it sounds good if the context in the original bears no relation to the new.

T.S. Eliot for instance was masterly at recycling bits of older poems, but the effect is always very carefully calculated. His quotation or deliberate misquotation is often a device to counterpoint differing values. Take, for example, these few lines from *The Waste Land;* III 'The Fire Sermon'.

The nymphs are departed.
Sweet Thames, run softly, till I end my song.
The river bears no empty bottles, sandwich papers,
Silk handkerchiefs, cardboard boxes, cigarette ends
Or other testimony of summer nights. The nymphs are departed.
And their friends, the loitering heirs of City directors;
Departed, have left no addresses.
By the Waters of Leman I sat down and wept ...
Sweet Thames, run softly, till I end my song.
Sweet Thames, run softly, for I speak not loud or long.

Nymphs are classical, but now departed, taking the antique world with them. The 'heirs of City directors' contrast with them ironically, as they have gone too, leaving no [forwarding] address.

Sweet Thames... comes from Edmund Spenser's 'Prothalamion', a charming Elizabethan poem written in honour of a wedding, in which the poet strolls along the banks of an older Thames from which the nymphs had *not* departed, and

Whose rutty Bancke, the which his Riuer hemmes,
Was paynted all with variable flowers,
And all the meades adornd with daintie gemmes,
Fit to decke maydens bowres.

The contrast between this Thames and the one filled with rubbish on summer nights is apparent. 'Waters of Leman' flow rather crookedly from Babylon to Switzerland, via the Prayer Book, more or less. The thought of exile is evoked. The whole fabric of meaning stated and meaning echoed is of a piece, that is regret for a vanished and better time.

If you make allusions like this, you must be very sure of the quality of your own writing, because you immediately invite comparison with the quoted poet. You can hitch a ride a little way, adding the wings of a famous line to your own - but a beginner takes a risk that the wax will melt and he may fall, like Icarus, into the sea.

Pre-existing stories

Huge numbers of poets freely use well-known episodes from history, stories, myths, and fairy-tales as skeleton frames for their own expression. Poets have always borrowed from religion, philosophy, chronicles, fireside tales, the anecdotes told by their friends ... The advantage is that you have a starting point, common ground between yourself and your reader. You can then adapt, change, surprise as you wish, with the original, expected story running in counterpoint beneath what you want to say. You don't have to waste effort in thinking of an original plot, if there is one ready for use.

Because education in the past included Greek and Latin, the classical myths, together with stories from the Bible, have been favourite sources for many centuries, but there is no reason why other myths and legends shouldn't be used.

Examples jump at you. Chaucer borrowed from French and Italian models, Shakespeare retold the story of Venus and Adonis, not to mention adapting Holinshed for the plots of his history plays. Milton rewrote *The Book of Genesis.* Tennyson recast Malory and other medieval romances in telling the story of King Arthur's Knights for a Victorian audience. The same material was treated quite differently by Charles Williams in his Arthurian poetry in this century.

The practice continues. Historical material was used in Byron's 'Destruction of Sennacherib', in Yeat's 'Easter 1916' and in a most individual way in Edith Sitwell's 'Anne Boleyn's Song'. A recently reported find in a Scandinavian peat-bog was the basis for Seamus Heaney's 'Tollund Man'.

Classical myth and legend have not yet been discarded, despite the near disappearance of the classics from our schools. Rayner Heppenstall had a psychological interpretation of the story of 'Actaeon', changed to a stag - or was he? - after seeing Artemis bathing. Auden gave a modern interpretation of the myth of 'Atlantis', and David Gascoyne followed 'Orpheus in the Underworld':

And he came carrying the shattered lyre,
And wearing the blue robes of a king.
And looking through eyes like holes torn in a screen.

The Bible, too, goes on giving generously, most famously perhaps in Eliot's 'The Journey of the Magi'.

Plagiarism

Anyone is allowed to quote from long-dead authors, but it is NOT permitted to lift lines from writers whose work is still in copyright. To steal someone else's work is as dishonest as to steal a credit card. If you quote from a writer still living or dead for less than fifty years you must acknowledge it and ask permission from the publisher. Copyright applies to the words themselves, not the ideas they express. For example, provided you use your own words, you are free to write anything you like about winter, though half the poets in the world have done so before you.

Folklore and legends have been used, but not overused yet. Walter de la Mare retold the persistent legend of 'Sunk Lyonesse', Thomas Hennell tells the story of 'A Mermaiden', said to have been cast up in Cornwall, and R.S. Thomas goes to Celtic mythology for 'The Ancients of the World'.

So all these marvellous sources are ready, waiting for you to renew them, to hand on to coming generations of readers the enduring or changing meanings they contain. No poet could wish for better, or more.

PRACTICAL WRITING

1. Look at your poem about a walk in the country or a park. Using this (or a new one), change half the images into ones employing synaesthesia. Try to vary the senses, so that you have vision in terms of sound, sound in terms of touch, touch in terms of smell

perhaps, and so on.

2. Write an allegory in a regular metrical form. E.g. a ballad telling the story of a search for someone or something, which has an underlying meaning of a quest for an abstract quality you value, such as truth, love etc.

3. Think of a few similes, as you have done before. Convert them to metaphors. Choose the one which lends itself to becoming an extended metaphor, and write a short poem using this or an elaborate conceit if you prefer. (Difficult, optional) Now eliminate all reference to the tenor of the metaphor. Have you some image left which can be used as a symbol? If so, write a short poem using it to imply several meanings;
e.g. Hatred is like wearing dark glasses. [simile]
Hatred is a dark glass between the sight and sun. [metaphor]
A poem entitled 'Hate' or 'Hatred' which actually describes all the dark kinds of glass you might see through: sunglasses, dirty windows, cracked telescopes... [extended metaphor]
A poem titled 'Black Glass', which might have to do with many different negative emotions or perceptions. [symbol]

(You might want to work in the Biblical reference too, of seeing 'through a glass, darkly', if it would be appropriate.)

4. a) Find a common symbol that attracts you, such as day/night, rose (love, perfection), water (purity, life), apple (fertility, home comfort in a pie or Eden's temptation). Write a poem with this as the central image, to convey its obvious meaning.
b) Choose another, similar symbol, but allow it to speak of your own concerns.
c) (Optional) If you are aware of any personal symbols, write the poem(s) that will embody your feelings.
d) (Optional) What mood are you in at present? Happy, sad, hopeful? Whatever it is, what caused it? Use the facts in a poem to try to evoke the same mood in a reader.

5. What is your favourite fairy-story, legend or myth? What does its imagery or message mean to you? Retell it in a suitable form, with or without rhyme, to make the meaning clear to someone else.

CHAPTER 9

SECRET PATTERNS

Poetry is a fusion between sound and sense. So far in this book a great deal of attention has been paid to subject-matter and imagery, with only basic regard to word-music, rhythm and rhyme. Now I want to describe some of the more subtle ways in which the sounds of language can be used to make verse memorable.

Word-Music

If rhythm gives life to poetry, the weaving of sound is its soul. Full rhymes at line-endings provide the most obvious pattern, followed by half-rhymes, but if you look closely at any really good poem you will find a further web: of rhymes in unexpected places, echoes, chimes, repetitions, dissonances, and other effects as complicated as a musical score. Yet because they work subconsciously, or subliminally, until these devices are pointed out they may not be noticed at all. Of course you can't add them to your kit of tools until you understand them.

The music of words can be found in prose too. When it is well composed, one feels instinctively that the piece is 'poetic'. Prose-poems exploit it, and it occurs in sacred writing. For instance, listen to part of Psalm 137 from the Authorised Version, set out as if it were free verse:

By the rivers of Babylon, there we sat down,
yea, we wept, when we remembered Zion.
We hanged our harps upon the willows
in the midst thereof.
For there they that carried us away captive
required of us a song; and they that wasted us
required of us mirth, saying,

Sing us one of the songs of Zion.
How shall we sing the Lord's song in a strange land?

This has several of the patterns I want to point out to you. There is near-rhyme, or at least echo: *Babylon/down/Zion*, and later *song/saying/sing/songs/Zion/sing/song.* Initial sounds of words are repeated: *By...Babylon; we wept when we... willows...wasted; hanged...harps; there they that; carried... captive; Lord's...land.* There is exact repetition of *required of us,* and variation in the last line of the one before it.

Now your turn. Read the following passage aloud and decide what special effects have been built in. (Never mind the meaning for once.)

As kingfishers catch fire, dragonflies draw flame;
As tumbled over rim in roundy wells
Stones ring; like each tucked string tells, each hung bell's
Bow swung finds tongue to fling out broad its name;
Each mortal thing does one thing and the same;
Deals out that being indoors each one dwells;
Selves - goes itself; myself it speaks and spells;
Crying What I do is me: for that I came.

(Hopkins, from 'As kingfishers catch fire')

I chose this because the sound-effects are comparatively obvious. For a start, you must have noticed the rhyme at the line-endings (it is the octave of a sonnet, rhyming *abba abba*) Did you spot the extra rhyme in line 3 - *tells/bell's*? Other sequences of full rhymes occur inside lines 1, 3, 4, 5 and 6: *king-/ring/string/fling/thing/(being)* and *hung/swung/tongue* and these sequences are half-rhymes with each other. There is internal consonance in *flame/tumbled/rim* in lines 1 and 2, and *dragon-/stones/ring...*Can you find more?

Alliteration and cynghanedd

Did a pattern in the first line strike you? Look at the whole again, with some of the sounds emphasised:

As kingfishers catch fire, dragonflies draw flame
K F SH K CH F DR FL DR FL M
As tumbled over rim in roundy wells
M R M R L
Stones ring; like each tucked string tells, each hung bell's
ST R L T STR T L B L
Bow swung finds tongue to fling out broad its name
B SW F T T FL BR M
Each mortal thing does one thing and the same
M TH TH M
Deals out that being indoors each one dwells;
D LZ TH B D Z DW LZ
Selves – goes itself; *myself* it speaks and spells;
S LV Z Z S LF M S LF SP K SP LZ
Crying *What I do is me: for that I came.*
KR D M F TH K M

Now let's reduce this to the sounds alone, dealing with consonants at the moment. Vowels will get their turn later on.

K F SH K CH F DR FL DR FL M
M R M R L
ST R L T STR T L B L
B SW F T T FL BR M
M TH TH M
D LZ TH B D Z DW LZ
S LV Z Z S LF M S LF SP K SP LZ
KR D M F TH K M

Such repeated clusters, line by line, aren't accidental, though they may come fairly easily to a poet once the inner ear knows what to listen for.

The repetition of a single initial sound at the beginning of several words close together is called *alliteration,* as in the Biblical passage (also in many advertising slogans, incidentally). A pattern of different sounds repeated, as in 'King Fishers Catch Fire', K F, K F, in the first line above, is a feature of Welsh poetry, and has the Welsh name *cynghanedd* (pronounced 'kunghanneth'). In Welsh prosody there are strict rules about it, but in English whatever works is fine. A variation is to repeat the sounds but in reverse order – instead of K F, K F you could have K F, F K for instance. Vowels can alliterate as well as consonants, and in some systems any initial vowel is deemed to alliterate with any other. Notice that we're talking about SOUNDS, of course. The spelling may or may not use the same letter.

Echoing consonants

More subtle and less noticeable than alliteration and cynghanedd is the effect when repeated sounds occupy different positions in several words close to each other. Let's call them 'echoing consonants'. For instance in 'Be bloody, bold and resolute,' the repeated *b* is clear, but what about the *l* and *d* with *t* close in sound as well? Be BLooDy BoLD anD resoLu(T)e, with the pattern B BL D B LD D .. L (T). (And did you notice that *be* and *bloody* are also rhymes, though the stress falls on one and not the other?)

There are many words you can use thus, with an intrusive vowel between the repeating consonants to give variety, as for instance *blow/below/billow/blue/ball, sly/silly, flit/fault/fillet, skewer/secure.*

Then you can have fun with to-and-fro sequences, such as *gore/rogue, reversed/deserve, still/lightest* and so on.

Consonant groups

More faintly echoing still, but still echoing, are sounds from the same phonetic grouping clustered together, the *d* and *t* sounds above, for instance. Phonetics is a subject for a degree course, and I've only a few paragraphs here, but this will give you a start.

Phonetic groups are based on the way the sounds are produced by lips, tongue and so on. If you say *pat* and *bat* you can feel the *p* and *b* sounds are made with only a small difference between them, hence they belong to the same group. Can you hear that *barber/people, beep* and *pub* all have a chiming effect?

Consonants

The consonantal groups are these:

1. *Plosives* (think of explosives) P B; T D; K G. All these have some affinity, but the paired sounds are closer to each other than to the rest.
2. *Nasal sounds* M N NG (as in 'sing').
3. L is alone, but there are two sounds, as in 'lily' and 'full'.
4. *Fricatives* (think of friction) F V; TH as in 'thin' and TH as in 'that'; R; H; S as in 'sea' and 'city' and Z in 'zoo'; SH as in 'she' and ZH, a sound like the French 'je', the sound in 'treasure'. These last two are allied also to:
5. *Affricatives* CH as in 'chap' and J as in 'junk'.

Finally:

6 *Semi-vowels* Y as in 'you' and W as in 'way'. Y goes well with J and ZH, and W with F and V sounds.

To remember the groupings can be really helpful when you are casting about for the right sound, especially if you want an echo to connect two words or ideas. But the right sound is often one from a different group, because as with rhyme, too much of anything can become tedious, like a tune on only three notes. The possible effects include contrast and transition as well as similarity. It is control of the network that makes the music.

Look at this, to see it in action:

An aged man is but a paltry thing,
  2 5 1 2 2 4 1 1 1 314 4 2   many plosives/nasals
A tattered coat upon a stick, unless
  1 1 1 1 1 1 2 41 1 23 4   mostly posives

Soul clap its hands and sing, and louder sing
4 3 13 1 14 4 214 21 4 2 21 3 1 4 2 mixed, with nasals
For every tatter in its mortal dress,
4 4 4 1 1 2 14 2 1 3 14 4 fricatives/plosives
Nor is there singing school but studying
2 4 4 4 2 2 41 3 1 1 41 16 2 mixed
Monuments of its own magnificence;
2 2 2 214 4 14 2 2 12 4 4 24 many nasals
And therefore I have sailed the seas and come
21 4 4 4 4 4 3 1 4 4 4 21 1 2 mostly fricatives
To the holy city of Byzantium.
1 4 4 3 41 4 1 4 21 2 plosives/fricatives, nasals.
(W.B.Yeats, from 'Sailing to Byzantium')

If you look at it from the point of view of dominant groups, you'll see how many energetic plosives there are, mixed with the singing effect of the nasals. The last line but one is mainly made of fricatives, with a fairly neutral effect until the last words which pick up the nasals again, preparing for the climax of *Byzantium*, the last word of the stanza, which encapsulates the mainly plosive/nasal pattern of the stanza as a whole.

You may notice too the large number of *t* and *s* sounds and the alliterative *m* in *Monuments of its own magnificence,* which is repeated in the important *come* and *Byzantium.*

In the following, there is a pattern of plosives with a dry rattle of fricatives in the background:

The silver birches are on fire
4 434 1 5 4 2 4 1 plosive
With a thin gold flame;
6 4 4 2 1 31 43 2 2 plosives
The sharp leaves of the briar
4 4 1 3 4 4 4 4 1 4 2 plosives
Burn with a russet gleam;
1 2 6 4 4 4 1 13 2 3 plosives

The bramble rough with red
4 14 213 4 4 6 4 4 1 3 plosives
Is a smouldering ember
4 42 31 4 2 21 2 plosives
And beeches though they soon will blaze
21 1 5 4 4 4 4 2 6 3 13 4 3 plosives
As yet are amber.
4 6 1 2 1 2 plosives

(John Smith, from 'Slow-Burning Autumn')

If you look at it from the point of view of dominant consonants, you'll see the repeated *b* and *r* sounds: *birches/briar/burn/bramble/ember/beeches/blaze/amber.* Alliterative *r* occurs in *russet/rough/red* and there is a quiet undercurrent of *f* and *l* too: *fire/flame/leaves/gleam/smouldering/will/blaze.* There is an echo in *gold/gleam* as well, and I haven't yet mentioned the half-rhymes, nor the vowel sounds ...

Here are a few more examples of poetry's music for you to practise on, to notice the rhymes, alliteration, cynghannedd and echoing consonants, and to work out the phonetic groupings if you wish:

Come buy, come buy:
Our grapes fresh from the vine,
Pomegranates full and fine,
Dates and sharp bullaces,
Rare pears and greengages,
Damsons and bilberries,
Taste them and try:
Currants and gooseberries,
Bright-fire-like barberries,
Figs to fill your mouth,
Citrons from the South,
Sweet to tongue and sound to eye;
Come buy, come buy.
(Christina Rossetti, from 'Goblin Market')

In a coign of the cliff between lowland and highland,
At the sea-down's edge between windward and lee,
Walled round with rocks as an inland island,
The ghost of a garden fronts the sea.
A girdle of brushwood and thorn encloses
The steep square slope of the blossomless bed
Where the weeds that grew green from the graves of its roses
Now lie dead.
(Algernon Swinburne, from 'A Forsaken Garden')

Bent double, like old beggars under sacks,
Knock-kneed, coughing like hags, we cursed through sludge...
(Wilfred Owen, from 'Dulce et Decorum Est')

Vowel sounds

The sounds of vowels and diphthongs are possibly even more important than the consonants, for they have a great deal to do with the pace of the line, whether it goes fast or slow. In a famous sonnet, the French poet Rimbaud (1854–1891) heard the vowels as colours – perhaps an example of synaesthesia, or perhaps a reference to alchemy. Anyway, getting the vowel sounds right, as well as the consonants, will change a leaden poem into gold.

One important consideration is length.
Long vowels : the sounds in *feet, food, farm, form, fern*
Diphthongs are long as well, as they are made from two short vowels sliding together, as in *ale, isle, oil; no, now; deer, dare, doer;* and *power, higher, mayor* with a neutral *e* added on.

Short vowels : as in *sit, set, sat, hut, hot, hood* and unaccented *the* or the last sound in *sofa*.

Precisely how long or short vowels are depends on the company they keep – *need* for instance is longer than *neat.*

Do you remember in Chapter Two, there were two extracts from Tennyson's 'The Lady of Shalott'? The first describes the river and island at the start of the story, the second after the magic mirror has cracked, when the Lady finds the boat to take her, dying, towards Camelot. The mood of each part is quite distinct, and I asked if you could discover differences in the sounds of the two pieces. I particularly had in mind the effects of the vowels.

Willows whiten, aspens quiver,	6 short, 2 diph.
Little breezes dusk and shiver	6 short, 1 long
Thro' the wave that runs for ever	5 short, 2 long, 1 diph.
By the island in the river	6 short 2 diph.
Flowing down to Camelot.	5 short, 2 diph.

Lots of short vowels, aren't there? *Willows, quiver, little, shiver, river* keep repeating the short *i*. Long sounds do occur in *whiten, breezes, wave, by* and *island,* but they are spaced out until two diphthongs close together slow the current, so to speak, in *Flowing down*. On the whole, the lines dance lightly. Now contrast this:

In the stormy east-wind straining,	5 short, 2 long, 1 diph.
The pale yellow woods were waning,	4 short, 1 long, 3 diph.
The broad stream in his bank complaining,	6 short, 2 long, 1 diph.
Heavily the low sky raining	5 short, 3 diph.
Over tower'd Camelot ...	4 short, 2 diph.

Because it takes longer to say the words, and hence the lines, I think there is an impression of uneasiness, just what the poet wanted at this point in his narrative.

Length is not the only thing to consider, either. When you speak, the vowel-sounds vary partly because of the position of the tongue in the mouth. As you might expect, the vowels are labelled *front, central* and *back.* In the variety of English called 'received pronunciation' these are:-

Front vowels: as in *feed, fit, met, mat.*
Central: as in *fern, the* (unstressed), *hut.*
Back: as in *mast, not, ford, put, mood.*
Diphthongs have affinities with both the sounds that make

them, *eye* for instance, sliding between the vowels of *mat* and *fit*. My own ear suggests that those containing the *fit* sound, as in *day, light, boy, ear* belong with the front vowels, *air, no* with the central, and *truer, now* with the back.

It is arguable that front vowels tend to give a lighter and more cheerful feeling to a line than the solemn, gloomier central and back ones, though this may be simply the associations of words such as *light, cheerful* and *solemn, gloomy*! This is a matter of opinion, not proven, but I suggest there is a difference in sound-association that reinforces the meaning in some words at least. A *lad* is less pompous than a *lord*, to *grin* is happier than to *groan* and a *feather* less significant than *father.* There is a difference between *little* and *large, high* and *low, light* and *dark.* (The heavier, sonorous vowels are long as well.) On the other hand, it doesn't always work – *noon* and *night* are the 'wrong' way round. I leave you to draw up your own list, and agree or disagree as you like. If there is anything in the idea, it will probably depend on the cumulative effect of several front, back or central vowels in line or stanza, and the contrasts between them, than on single words.

Onomatopoeia

This brings me to the subject of *onomatopoeia.*

There are undoubtedly some words which deliberately copy natural sounds: *cuckoo, bow-wow, tweet, moo, miaow, purr, squeak, squawk* from the conversation of birds and animals, *splash, squelch, thud, bang, boom* from impact or explosion, *pop, rip, snap, crack* when things break. All these and many others are useful when you want to evoke the experience.

But onomatopoeia in poetry means more than using such words.

> *Tis not enough no harshness gives offence,*
> *The sound must seem an echo to the sense:*
> *Soft is the strain when Zephyr gently blows,*
> *And the smooth stream in smoother numbers flows,*
> *But when loud surges lash the sounding shore,*

The hoarse, rough verse should like the torrent roar.
When Ajax strives some rock's vast weight to throw,
The line too labours, and the words move slow:
Not so when swift Camilla scours the plain,
Flies o'er the unbending corn, and skims along the main.
(Pope, from *An Essay on Criticism* lines 364–373)

This famous passage not only states but exemplifies all it says. Read it aloud. How does it get its different effects, all within the constraints of rhyming iambic couplets, even with an extra foot in the last line? Take a few minutes and work it out, analysing, for instance, the pace given by long and short vowels, the consonant clusters that cannot be pronounced quickly in the *Ajax* line, the alliteration, consonance, assonance, the effect of the different types of consonants ...

All very well when your images have to do with sounds and movement. But perhaps you are writing about something like a nervous breakdown? Could you suggest this by disjointed rhythm, slow-moving lines, and dissonant consonant clusters, especially fricatives and affricatives mixed with a few plosives? A requiem? You will probably reach into your mind's ear for words with back-vowels. Or a poem about fire? Try using a lot of front-vowel sounds to suggest light, and words such as flicker, flame, flash, flare, which seem individually onomatopoeic. For water-music you will need liquid *l*s and perhaps murmuring *m*s. The hiss of steam, snake or malice is easy to suggest, but take care not to use too many sibilants in quiet, friendly poems.

Do such correspondences really exist in language? Or have they been invented by people needing the reassurance of finding logical patterns in apparent chaos? I believe they are real to some extent, but being far less obvious than the meaning of words, they can easily be overridden.

The ideal is to make sound and meaning work together, which you can do only by trial and error when you begin to write. You can't think of everything at once, and many poets will be considering the imagery to start with – 'I want something about a shattered glass here', not 'I need a plosive and front vowels followed by some fricatives, falling to nasals and low back vowels'. The labels are merely signposts. You need to study the road for yourself, so that you take the right turning without thinking about it. Or to put it another way, there is a magical tradition that sounds have occult properties. In poetry at least this is true. Now you know some of the secret spells, but how you use them is up to you. Your discoveries and enchantments must be your own.

PRACTICAL WORK

1. Write down a stanza or two of a poem which you like and know by heart, leaving space between the lines. Go through it carefully, noting down any of the devices mentioned in this chapter. Is the poem onomatopoeic in a literal or more general way? Do you think any of the techniques of alliteration etc. help to make it memorable, or not?

2. Repeat the above with a poem completely new to you. Does the poet seem to be paying more attention to imagery, or sound, or is there a balance between the two? Do any

particularly inappropriate sounds strike you? Does the poem sound especially melodious or harsh? Why? (This kind of analysis will teach you a great deal, but don't let it spoil your simple enjoyment of poetry by inhibiting your gut responses.)

3. Find a poem among the ones you have already written which has something wrong with it, as in exercise 1 of Chapter Seven. Go through the checklist for constructive criticism suggested there, and add a very careful consideration of word-music to the list. Make this a habit too when you revise work in future.

4. Abandon the meaning of words altogether (if you can) and write poems with sounds and rhythm to evoke a) a summer day in the country, b) a journey on a motorway, perhaps with an accident or delay, c) a concert of your favourite kind of music, d) living in a foreign country where you don't know the language.

5. Return to meaning, and write a short poem to do with a river-trip, ferry crossing, afternoon in a punt or other watery occasion, making the imagery and sound work together as closely as possible.
(More difficult) Write another to do with being in hospital, as patient, visitor or member of staff. Try to suggest the clinical atmosphere through both sound and imagery.

6. Write a dramatic dialogue between a contrasting pair of people – e.g. child and headmaster, apprentice and managing director, dancer and weightlifter. Use an appropriate register for each person, and also try to include many short and front vowels for the first, long and back vowels for the second.

7. Look at the poems you wrote using symbolism, exercise 4 in Chapter Eight. Do the sounds and rhythm of your words adequately echo the symbols you chose? Repeat the exercise, taking particular care of this aspect. E.g. If you choose a bell as symbol, you might want to suggest its tolling; or an animal's sound or movement; or a heavy object's static quality.

CHAPTER 10

WHAT'S IN IT FOR YOU?

I began this book by saying that poetry is important for society at large, from which it follows that as society changes, new poets are always needed, the singers and seers required to interpret a group or nation's myths. The more people who know even a little about poetry and who practise it, even if only as an occasional interest, the greater the civilising influence will be.

But what does the individual gain from writing it? What do *you* want from poetry? How much time and creativity can you devote to it? As with a building, the house depends on the number of bricks you invest in it. However, there is no need to sign your name in blood on a Conveyance of Dedication unless you want to. There are all grades of commitment from full time vocation (but how are you going to eat?), to a lighthearted attempt at a poem once or twice a year. Besides, if you are a beginner you won't yet know exactly how important poetry is going to be to you. You may even decide not to write yourself, but to be the valuable, informed listener, the necessary counterpart of the poet.

But if you have read this far, I assume you are still interested in writing regularly. Doing anything creative is a source of delight. If you have talent, it's a waste, even a wicked waste, not to develop it. Once you have done your best with a poem, you have made something that you alone can make, and nothing is more satisfying than that.

That is just the beginning. Writing brings other benefits. Practice makes you better at it, and as fluency improves you communicate more easily, saying more exactly what you mean. Skilful writing is invaluable in many kinds of work and in social life too.

Using your imagination, as even the humblest poet must,

also gives bonuses in life. The more you can put yourself in another's place the more you will understand different view-points and be better able to make sympathetic choices. A strong imagination helps you in other ways as well. It can lead you to become the kind of person you would like to be. It encourages you to see new solutions to practical problems. It lets you go on mini-holidays otherwhen and elsewhere if you can spare a few minutes away from present time, to which you will return refreshed. There is no need to escape with drugs or alcohol if your own mind can supply adventurous psychedelic trips all by itself - cheaply and safely too.

Poetry can be the valve on an emotional pressure-cooker, hissing out dangerous steam when the heat is on. To express feelings such as fear, anger and frustration, without hurting anyone or smashing plates, can help you to use destructive energy for better ends. Interesting self-analysis is possible from studying the drift of your individual symbolism when you are in an objective mood. Some people are greatly comforted by using poetry as therapy, maybe with traditional forms as safe and limiting frames for painful memories. A persona lets you off the hook as well. Using a mask enables you to express all kinds of stuff that your 'real' self might not be able to explore directly.

However, there is a down-train on the line too, carrying you into solitude. You have to be prepared to be abstracted from family, friends, partner, or children as you write, even if you are physically sitting at the same kitchen-table. This is apt to irritate those who don't share your interests. It's just as well to be aware of this, so you can work out what to do about opposition or jealousy if you encounter them.

From your own point of view, this loneliness can turn into real grief if you have no-one to share with. For reasons which I've already glanced at, poets are sometimes regarded patron-isingly or dismissively. 'Poetry? Bit wet (daft/sissy/ airy-fairy) innit?' It can be a great relief to join a workshop, creative writing class, or writers' circle, so that you meet others like yourself and realise that you haven't actually got snakes in your hair or three noses. Besides, informed and constructive criticism is probably the best gift you can be given, and it can be bestowed only by those as good as you, or better. Don't however stay with a group if you don't feel happy there after a reasonable trial period. Move on, or start your own. Poets can be vulnerable, especially at the beginning of their careers, and the wrong atmosphere can be harmful.

Nobody today can expect to become rich from writing poetry. If there is nothing in your wallet, but money is on your mind, go away and do something else to earn it. Poetry is not a job, although it is work. Even the most successful poets usually have some other means of paying for their trips to the supermarket. Some can write novels, or work in radio, television, advertising, McDonald's, a bank; or as housewives, teachers, clerks, nannies, priests, postmen, actors, civil servants; anything. (If you're on the dole, you can make the most of it in verse.) Most poets are part-timers, writing in the evenings, on buses, on holiday; and earning, possibly, a little pocket money from magazines or poetry-readings.

The same applies to fame. How good are you, really? If you're just starting out, you can't tell. There are many competent poets who give pleasure to others and themselves, but only a very few will be asked for autographs by strangers in the street. This doesn't mean that effort is wasted and talent ignored. If you are a true poet, part of the work is to share with others. A poem is only half alive until it is heard or read. Modest success is perfectly possible if you keep writing, keep improving, and keep submitting work for publication. And until you try, how can you find out if you are a sparrow or a golden eagle?

Trying to get published

There are many 'little' magazines which welcome new writers, and established ones which will take very good work. Look in *The Writers' and Artists' Yearbook* or *The Writers' Handbook* for a list of magazines which print poetry, and much useful advice besides. Look at poetry departments in bookshops. Buy a magazine which publishes your kind of verse. One will often lead you to others. Public libraries are helpful too.

When you have researched possible magazine homes for your work, make your poems look neat and tidy to give them a good chance. They really must be freshly typed, or crisply photocopied, on A4 paper, one poem to a page, with your name and address on each.

An absolute rule is NEVER SEND THE ONLY COPY OF A POEM AWAY. Keep master-copies in a file at home, so it won't be a disaster if someone's dog eats the post.

Find out the editor's name from the magazine itself, a reference book, or possibly a phone call, and send this person a SHORT covering letter, offering your work for publication. Confirm that it is original and unpublished (or say where it was published before). No biographical details yet. Your poems must speak up for themselves.

Enclose a stamped envelope, addressed to yourself, or international reply coupons if sending abroad. This is important, as small magazines can't afford large postage bills, and won't send back unsolicited poems unless they have an s.a.e.

You need to know what is happening to your work. Keep a record of submissions in a notebook, like a postage book, with date, names of poems sent, where sent, and a space for the result. Then you can check you aren't sending the same poem twice to the same editor.

After that, write some more, send them out too, and keep going. It is bad etiquette to send the same poems to more than one editor at a time, just in case both accept your work. But a more likely outcome is that your poems will flutter back to you, several weeks or even months later, accompanied by a standard rejection slip. 'The Editor regrets' etc.

A rejection slip is disappointing. Those were your best poems and now they've been turned down. It's natural to feel discouraged, so feel discouraged for a few minutes, but then tell yourself that it's your poems that have been rejected, not you personally. Your own worth is not affected. Editors get far more poems than they can possibly publish, so some have to be sent back. Perhaps the editor had a hangover and couldn't appreciate your work properly. Perhaps ...

Sometimes a little personal note will be added – 'Enjoyed these, but don't think they're quite right for *Blah.* Best wishes.' It means you're making progress. Send this editor some more poems after a decent interval.

But however a rejection comes, this is what to do. Read the poems again. Do *you* still like them? If so, check they aren't dog-eared (or chewed!) and send them to another editor. Write some more and better ones. Send them out. Write some more and send them out ...

Regard an acceptance as a triumph, but (I'm rubbing it in) most poetry magazines don't pay anything. They usually send you a free copy or two of the issue in which your poem appears. Photocopy the poem as well as holding on to the magazine and keep a scrapbook of your work. Record the happy date in your notebook. When you see your first poem published, you'll think that you'll never forget the day, but after half-a-dozen you get more blasé.

Magazines aren't the only outlets for poems either. You can sometimes get yourself invited to perform your work at various functions, such as pub-readings, political meetings, parties and so on. Again, most of these opportunities will be unpaid, but you will be sharing your gifts with an audience.

Local and national radio programmes are also a possibility. Listen first, to see if your work is anything like what is broadcast. Submit poems to the producer as for a magazine, offering to read them if you possibly can.

Book publication

Many people will find that modest recognition is sufficient but some will feel talented enough to go further.

Getting a collection published is a long-term ambition. When you have had a number of poems in magazines or on radio, you can select your best work and submit it to poetry book publishers. In principle it's the same as sending your work to magazines, but higher up on the spiral. If you receive standard rejection letters at first, keep going as before.

Producing small booklets by desk-top publishing is another possibility, until a breakthrough comes. Prepare a neat copy of the poems on the right size of paper and in page sequence, using a computer and word-processing software. Take the master-copy round local print shops to compare estimates. Perhaps you could join with several others to do this, and share costs, the work of editing, keying in the text and so on. You all have to be prepared to be salespeople too, but if you produce about 100 booklets, for instance, at a production cost of perhaps £200, and you have a lot of friends, you may manage to break even.

Avoid advertisers in newspapers and writing magazines who ask for poetry to be sent to them. It's highly likely they belong to the vanity press. Your poems will be praised uncritically, you will be asked to pay for publication - and the book won't get serious attention from anyone. Bookshops will be chary of stocking it. Many copies may end up pulped. You will have wasted a lot of money.

Self-publishing is somewhat different. You go into business on your own account, and will succeed or fail according to your business sense, time, capital etc. as well as the perceived worth of your poetry. You need to look into it very carefully so that you know what you're letting yourself in for. It's probably more sensible to try for several years to get published by someone else before you contemplate this step. Desk-top publishing of small booklets is a good first move.

Competitions

Competitions are listed in the writers' guides mentioned already, and in some other publications such as *Writers News.* Winning gives tremendous encouragement, even better than having a poem published in a magazine. If you win a large competition you will also get a cash prize and a measure of fame, a bonus for your career. You might think it's a good idea to enter every competition you hear about.

Whether this is so depends firstly on the thickness of your skin, and secondly on the thickness of your wallet. A tough attitude is essential. There are literally thousands of entries for the major competitions, but usually only about three winners. The chances of even a brilliant poem succeeding are, let's say, one in a thousand. There will be nine hundred and ninety-nine disappointed poets out of every thousand who entered. The chances of getting published by submitting to magazines is much better than that.

It's also expensive to go in for a lot of competitions. A few are free but there is an entry fee for most, which can run to several pounds per poem. Would you do better to spend the money on ordinary postage? Or books? Or something else entirely? Only you know the answers. If you can enter with a 'nothing to lose by trying' attitude, and don't mind a flutter with your money, at least you'll get a bit of excitement.

Responsibilities

If you are a new poet, still perhaps struggling to remember the difference between iambs and trochees, the notion that what you write might alter history may seem bizarre. But as most poets do write for others as well as for their own satisfaction, you ought to consider, right at the start of your career, the power your words may have. A poem is a social act - or an Act if Shelley was right and poets are 'the unacknowledged legislators of the world', and the better the poem the more potent it will be.

You can think of a poem as a thought-form, mind-energy given a shape that takes on life of its own, and which goes on living even after the originator has forgotten it, or died. The reader of course has some responsibility for accepting or rejecting it, for allowing its influence or not. However, as poetry does often work on a subconscious level, a lucky thought-form may slip past the reader's guard occasionally.

What kind of influence do you want to have, perhaps even on people not yet born? If your work is going to be a force for good it must, I think, tell the truth, not in a narrow sense of its being Tuesday and not Friday when you fell in love, but in the deeper sense of being psychologically true. Poetry of complaint is easier to write than poetry of affirmation, but should not be written simply because it is easy, but only if it will purge wrong or pain. Celebratory poetry can be facile and sentimental, unless it is faithful to your own vision of goodness, whatever that may be.

(For the Finland-Swedish poet, Edith Södergran, 1892-1923, who kept faith in her words despite the critics)

Refusing the crown that would wreathe her as dumb,
my Northern-Sister comes, saying, `It does not

become me to make myself less than I am.'
And she moves into forest
and she brings me out handfuls of snow,
a rugged fir,
a taste of wild-thyme,
which is only a taste of her own joyousness –
the fearless gates she keeps open,
including the one for death.

(Grace Nichols, from 'My Northern-Sister')

Your responsibility as a poet is to be very sure that what you say is what you really believe, to express as skilfully as you can the essence of what you are.

The metaphor of a bag of tools is valid for the various ways of manipulating language in poetry, but only you can decide what you will make with the kit, whether it will be only a simple shelf, or a carving to be wondered at for a thousand years. Whatever it turns out to be, I wish you well.

CHECKLIST OF SUBJECTS

Subjects for poetry are as diverse as the contents of the Oxford Dictionary, because anything that happens in life, death or alternative universes can be your quarry.

Nevertheless, some topics are more popular than others. This short list may be helpful, if only to encourage you to spot omissions and think of more original categories:–

Great life events	birth
	love
	sex
	loss
	death
Emotional states	joy/triumph
	sadness/depression/grief
	exaltation
	anger/hatred
	fear
	love
	curiosity
	greed/lust
	envy
Personal interations with	kin/parents/children/ siblings
	friends
	enemies
	strangers
	bosses
	employers
	workmates
Society	life in town/country
	education/learning/ teaching/schools/ universities and their towns

	entertainment
	work/workers
	factories/offices
	outdoor work
	trades
	professions
	arts, etc.
	high life
	crime
	criminals/police
	poverty
	unemployment
	escape from others
	recluses
	desert islands
The body and its associations	parts of the body/internal organs
	food/meals
	sleep/dreams
	excretion
	accidents/illness/pain
	exercise/sport
	warmth/coldness/comfort
	clothes
Poet as witness	world of nature
	animals and habitats
	landscape
	weather
	urban life
	streetscapes
	shops
	traffic
The earth	ecology
	expoitation of the earth
	healing the earth
	geology
	weather

	natural wonders
	natural disasters
	ocean/seas/rivers
	forest/deserts
	farms/farming
	gardens/gardeners/fruit/ flowers/vegetables
Travelling	cars/trains/planes/ships/ spacecraft/rollerskates/ pogo sticks/bikes/ walking
	travel in same country
	contrasting environments
	foreign countries near and far
	different customs
	science fiction and fantasy lands
Staying put	home neighbourhood
	houses – interiors
	old buildings/ruins
Animals	wild and tame
	pets/zoos
	mammals
	birds
	fish
	reptiles
	insects (e.g. Donne's Flea)
	mankind as animals
War	politics
	combatants
	victims
	battles/victories/defeats
Religion	prayer/devotion
	personal response to your own god(s)

	criticism of abuses hymns
Mysticism, psychic phenomena	states of higher consciousness ESP/telepathy/clairvoyance ghosts/hauntings near-death/out-of-body experiences
Stories	myths/legends/Biblical (e.g. Milton) history/historical persons old stories told from another angle (e.g. Andromeda's view of Perseus
Science	technology machinery inventions/inventors specific sciences - e.g. astronomy old sciences e.g. alchemy
Crafts	well-known, such as pottery esoteric, such as carving buttons
Arts	fine arts/painting/music individual paintings individual musical works poetry itself artists/writers/musicians

BASICS

►A good *English dictionary,* as comprehensive as you can afford - THE CONCISE OXFORD DICTIONARY for example, published by Oxford University Press.
►*A guide to modern English usage.*
►At least one *anthology of modern verse* - see below.

These are the minimum. Add gradually to your collection as your needs grow. Some of the following are out of print, but can often be bought second-hand.

POETRY

►*Anthologies of verse* especially modern ones. There are a lot available. Here is a selection to choose from:-
►THE PENGUIN BOOK OF ENGLISH VERSE, edited by John Hayward, Penguin. A collection of traditional work, 1500 - 1950, useful for studying the roots of English poetry, or
►THE NEW OXFORD BOOK OF ENGLISH VERSE 1250 - 1950, chosen and edited by Helen Gardner, O.U.P. Covers much the same ground as the above, but rather more fully.
►THE RATTLE BAG, edited by Seamus Heaney & Ted Hughes, Faber & Faber. An attractive mixture of traditional and modern.
►IMAGIST POETRY. Introduced and edited by Peter Jones, Penguin.
►THE PENGUIN BOOK OF CONTEMPORARY BRITISH POETRY, edited by Blake Morrison and Andrew Motion, Penguin.
►THE NEW POETRY, edited by Michael Hulse, David Kennedy and David Morley, Bloodaxe Books. Right up to date.
►PENGUIN MODERN POETS. A series from 1 - 27 from the 1960s onwards, each containing work by three different poets.
►THE FABER BOOK OF TWENTIETH CENTURY VERSE: An Anthology of Verse in Britain 1900 - 1950, edited by John Heath-Stubbs and David Wright, Faber & Faber.
►THE OXFORD BOOK OF CONTEMPORARY VERSE 1945 - 1980, chosen by D.J. Enright, O.U.P.
►THE OXFORD BOOK OF TWENTIETH-CENTURY ENGLISH VERSE, chosen by Philip Larkin. O.U.P.
►THE NEW OXFORD BOOK OF LIGHT VERSE, chosen by Kingsley Amis, O.U.P.
And of course, individual works by your favourite poets.

REFERENCE

►A *thesaurus* which gives synonyms and related words.
►ROGET'S THESAURUS is the classic, or
►CHAMBERS 20TH CENTURY THESAURUS.
►*A guide to poetic forms.*
►THE POET'S MANUAL AND RHYMING DICTIONARY, by Frances Stillman, Thames & Hudson, is very helpful. The rhyming dictionary section will save many chewed pencil-ends. And/or
►HOW TO BE WELL-VERSED IN POETRY compiled and edited by E.O. Parrott, Viking Press. Doubles as a guide to parody. The most entertaining work on prosody I've ever read.
►A book which lists *common symbols* such as
►A DICTIONARY OF SYMBOLS by Tom Chetwynd, Paladin. An attractive introduction to the subject. Or,
►AN ILLUSTRATED ENCYCLOPAEDIA OF TRADITIONAL SYMBOLS, by J.C. Cooper, Thames & Hudson, and/or
►SYMBOLIC AND MYTHOLOGICAL ANIMALS, by J.C. Cooper, Aquarian/Thorsons, or
►A DICTIONARY OF SYMBOLS, by J.E. Cirlot, translated from the Spanish by Jack Sage, Routledge & Kegan Paul. The most academic of this group.
►*A Guide to myths and legends* such as
►BREWER'S DICTIONARY OF PHRASE & FABLE, revised by Ivor H. Evans, Cassell, or BREWER'S MYTH AND LEGEND edited by J.C. Cooper. Handy for quick reference, or
►A DICTIONARY OF MYTHOLOGIES, compiled by Rhoda A. Hendricks, edited by Max S. Shapiro, Paladin.
►NEW LAROUSSE ENCYCLOPEDIA OF MYTHOLOGY, published by Hamlyn. A comprehensive outline of the world's myths.
These are merely three out of many possible choices.
►*Guides to the natural word* – flowers, trees, etc. such as those illustrated with photographs by Roger Phillips, published by Pan. These help to avoid embarrassing mistakes of fact.
►A book of *word games* to cheer you up when the going gets heavy, such as
►THE OXFORD GUIDE TO WORD GAMES, by Tony Augarde, O.U.P.

HELP WITH PUBLISHING

►THE WRITER'S HANDBOOK, edited by Barry Turner, Macmillan, published every year, or
►WRITERS' & ARTISTS' YEARBOOK, published annually by A. & C. Black.

▸HOW TO PUBLISH YOUR POETRY: A practical guide, by Peter Finch, Allison & Busby.

BOOKS ABOUT THE TECHNICAL ASPECTS OF POETRY (ADVANCED)

▸A POETRY HANDBOOK A Dictionary of Terms, by Babette Deutsch, Cape. An interesting collection of definitions and short articles.

▸HOW POETRY WORKS: The Elements of English Poetry, by Philip Davies Roberts, Penguin. Especially concerned with the sounds and stresses of poetry.

▸A LINGUISTIC GUIDE TO ENGLISH POETRY, by Geoffrey N. Leech, Longman. Very advanced study of language for the intellectual poet.

▸THE POETIC IMAGE, by C. Day Lewis, Jonathan Cape.

INDEX OF POETS QUOTED OR CITED

(those without dates are still alive)

GENERAL INDEX

OTHER PRAXIS TITLES FOR WRITERS

In Search of Life's Meaning
by Raymond Matley and Rebecca Smith.
Poets are philosophers, too. Here in one compendium volume is an overview of all the major and not-so-major approaches to the great questions of existence. Mysticism, feminism, Marxism, nihilism - and a great many more -isms are described in a light accessible style.
288 pages. Paperback. £7.50. ISBN 0-9518729-0-7

A Book of Folklore
by Sabine Baring-Gould.
A reissue of a classic collection of myths, legends, country practices, first published in 1913. The Reverend Baring-Gould was a great Victorian character, with many passionate interests. Folklore was a lifelong pursuit, and this book is a distillation of fifty years' collecting. Many stories are firsthand accounts from people who saw ghosts or used extraordinary remedies for their troubles. Inspiration for many a poem lies within these pages.
176 pages, including a new Introduction and Index. Paperback. £5.00
ISBN 0-9518729-4-X

Order through your bookshop, or send the form below to: Praxis Books, "Sheridan", Broomers Hill Lane, Pulborough, West Sussex. RH20 2DU.

Please send .... copies of *In Search of Life's Meaning*
.... copies of *A Book of Folklore*
(Cheques payable "Praxis Books". Add 75p for postage for 1 book, £1 for two).
to:
Name..
Address..
....
....
....